IMAGES
of America

BEACON
REVISITED

THE FIREMEN'S PARADE ALONG MAIN STREET. Spectators line Main Street for a 1971 firemen's parade. *Beacon Revisited* follows the authors' initial book of archival photographs from the 1870s to World War II, *Historic Beacon*, which concentrated on the traditional, fundamental chapters of the city's history. This new work is different is several ways: first, it focuses largely on the latter half of the 20th century; second, it is arranged thematically to celebrate the city's rebirth at the start of the 21st century as a center for the arts; and third, it presents an eclectic collection of images and anecdotes to reflect Beacon's unique sense of community spirit.

IMAGES
of America

BEACON
REVISITED

Robert J. Murphy
and Denise Doring VanBuren

ARCADIA
PUBLISHING

Published by Arcadia Publishing
Charleston, South Carolina

Library of Congress Catalog Card Number: 2003110755

For all general information contact Arcadia Publishing at:
Telephone 843-853-2070
Fax 843-853-0044
E-mail sales@arcadiapublishing.com
For customer service and orders:
Toll-Free 1-888-313-2665

Visit us on the Internet at www.arcadiapublishing.com

*To Beacon City Historian Joan Keating VanVoorhis—teacher,
friend, fellow enthusiast for Beacon's past.*

—R.J.M.

*In honor of my parents, who taught me a love of local history;
in appreciation to my sister-in-law Erin, who brought me to Beacon;
in gratitude to my associates at Central Hudson Gas & Electric
Corporation, who set the standard in community service;
and in debt to my sons, Schuyler, Troy, and Brett, and my husband,
Steve, who sacrifice so much to let me do the things I love.*

—D.D.VB.

CONTENTS

INTRODUCTION

Located just 60 miles north of Manhattan on one of the most scenic stretches of the Hudson River shoreline, the city of Beacon was born on May 15, 1913, with the merger of the adjoining villages of Fishkill Landing (a thriving river port) and Matteawan (a robust manufacturing center).

The twin villages and the combined city that followed are steeped in history: the site of the world famous Mount Beacon Incline Railway, location of one of the longest-running ferries in U.S. history, home to one of the Hudson River Valley's first electric streetcar systems, and birthplace of several prominent Americans. Beacon's setting at the majestic gate of the Hudson Highlands also made it the ideal location for several significant estates; its proximity to New York contributed to its economic and social status; its numerous factories were once nationally recognized for manufacturing dozens of products, most notably, hats.

Like many small cities in the Northeast, Beacon fell on difficult times during the latter half of the 20th century: factories closed, some families fled to the suburbs, and merchants boarded over Main Street windows. Somehow, although many neighborhoods fell into decline and few employers remained, the essence of Beacon was never completely extinguished and the spirit that sustained the city through the tough times buoyed Beacon into rebirth at the dawn of the 21th century.

The Tallix Art Foundry and the Dia Art Foundation have made Beacon one of the most notable addresses in the art world. Urban pioneers have rediscovered the beauty of the Hudson River Gothic Main Street and the strong, solid lines of factory buildings. Artisans and antique dealers have flocked to storefronts, and a new wave of settlers has restored block after block of Victorian homes. Families cannot resist Beacon's allure of good schools, close-knit neighborhoods, proximity to New York City, and scenic beauty.

Best of all, Beacon retains a committed sense of community spirit and diversity. James Forrestal, Beacon native and first U.S. secretary of defense, recognized it more than a half century ago and reflected on it when addressing the employees at the New York Rubber Company on October 18, 1943:

> Beacon and Dutchess County are as good an example as there is of what constitutes American life. We live in a valley richly endowed with the traditions of our country's beginnings. The names Washington, Hamilton, Schuyler, Verplanck, Chancellor Kent are great names both in the history of the country and of our own community.
>
> At the same time, this city and country are representative of the amalgam of peoples which has given this nation extraordinary growth and world power within a century. Both have in them descendants of immigrants of English, Scotch, and Irish extraction, of German, Dutch, Italian, Polish, Czech, and Balkan ancestry.
>
> I am proud of the fact that in this town the sons and daughters of these immigrants went to school together and played games together with children of older origins without thought of bigotry, bias or prejudice. There were, and probably still are, the jealousies and animosities which are part of the normal complexity of human relationships. But broadly speaking, the individual in this community, whether a descendant of the Dutch patroons, of the English colonials or the recently arrived immigrant, stood on his own feet and was judged as an individual on his own merits and character. . . .
>
> That is the Beacon in which the boys of our generation grew up, and I suspect it is still the Beacon of today. . . . There were Cornishmen like Henry Corney, Scotchmen like William Graham, Irishmen like John Mara, Jews like Samuel Beskin and David Alper, and men like my father and Edward St. John, all of whom had a deep sense of community responsibility and did their best to discharge it.
>
> That is the social and political national unit that is America. It is in a sense a miracle in human relationships. It is a miracle that is not understood by many outside this country. . . . It is the idea and the ideal that our men fight for today in many climes and in distant waters. . . . It is evidence that democracy is still a vibrant, vital and vigorous concept.

One

CONTEMPORARY

"Current; modern."

THE OPENING OF DIA: BEACON, 2003. On May 18, 2003, a new chapter in the city's evolution was unveiled with the formal dedication of Dia:Beacon, which hosts one of the world's largest and most distinguished collections of contemporary art. The museum, housed in a former Nabisco cardboard box–printing plant, boasts 300,000 square feet of expansive exhibit galleries. The overhead skylights, which once provided the natural illumination necessary to ensure uniformity in the package-printing process, now shower famous artworks with abundant natural light.

THE ENTRANCE TO DIA:BEACON, 2003. Artist Robert Irwin created the master plan for the 70-acre museum property, which includes an entrance marked with a grove of flowering trees, selected for their changing appearance over the seasons. The Dia Art Foundation, which was founded in 1974, derives its name from the Greek word meaning "through" and is dedicated to commissioning and supporting contemporary works of art (dating from the 1960s to the present). More than 60,000 art enthusiasts from around the world are expected to visit the Beacon location each year, and numerous independent galleries have sprung up along Main Street in anticipation of their arrival.

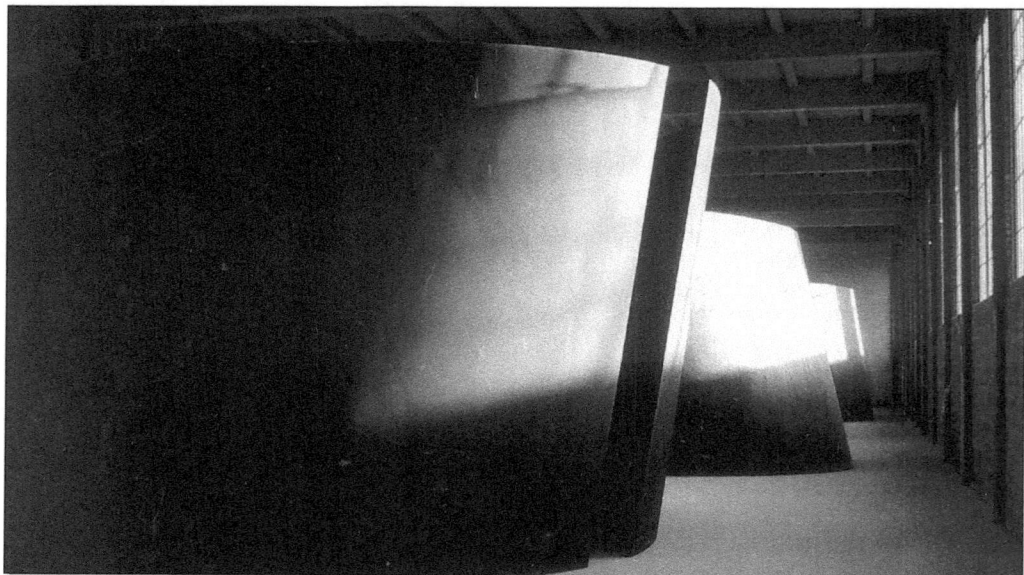

TORQUED ELLIPSE II, 1996; DOUBLE TORQUED ELLIPSE, 1997. Within the Dia:Beacon collection, these pieces by Richard Serra join a vast range of works by some of the most significant artists of the last half century, including Donald Judd, Andy Warhol, Dan Flavin, and John Chamberlain. Each gallery is devoted to a single artist, several of whom collaborated on the installation of their works.

A Pressman Inspecting Saltine Cracker Boxes, the 1950s. After its opening in 1929, the Nabisco printing and carton plant in Beacon produced hundreds of millions of cardboard boxes annually for Nabisco. At its peak in 1953, the Nabisco plant employed some 600 men and women, working in three shifts, to run the offset presses and the cutting and folding machines. In 1985, Nabisco sold the building to the Federal Paper Board Company, which continued printing cartons there until it closed in 1990.

Women Workers at Nabisco, c. the 1950s. One of the more tedious jobs at the Nabisco box and carton plant was that of the "pickers," women who, with hammers in hand, would swing away all day, knocking out the perforated pieces of cardboard that were part of the box construction process. An ameliorating feature of the Nabisco factory was the skylight system. With more than 40,000 square feet of glass, the natural light streaming down made for bright working conditions on the factory floor.

TALLIX ARTISANS, 1995. The Korean War Memorial, the Franklin Delano Roosevelt Memorial, and a giant horse may be the most famous of the works produced at the Tallix Art Foundry, but they are just three of hundreds of sculptures created in Beacon since Tallix arrived in 1986. Working in the Green Fan factory that once produced industrial equipment, artisans today use molds in a lost-wax process to create metal sculptures of all sizes, including the 19 seven-and-a-half-foot-tall stainless steel Korean War soldiers now at the National Mall in Washington, D.C.

IL CAVALLO CAST AT TALLIX, **1999.** *Il Cavallo* was cast at Tallix five centuries after the original clay model by Leonardo da Vinci was destroyed. The Italian master designed the 24-foot-high statue, but French soldiers used its model for target practice during the invasion of Milan in 1499. Determined to realize Leonardo's dream, a private foundation financed creation of the nearly 14-ton statue. Some 50,000 people marveled at it during a three-day June celebration in Beacon.
Il Cavallo was then shipped to Milan, where it was unveiled on September 10, 1999, as a gift to all Italians from the American people.

THE GREEN FUEL ECONOMIZER. An English firm that established its American base in 1891 in a Main Street factory near Herbert Street, the Green Fuel Economizer company initially specialized in economizers: tube systems that heat feed water for industrial boilers in order to increase efficiency. Within five years, the company prospered enough to purchase the estate of Peter Schenck, the father of this factory town, and, in time, expanded to six buildings.

THE GREEN FAN, 1952. Constructed beside the Newburgh, Dutchess & Connecticut Railroad, the Green Fan complex had ideal access to both raw materials and outbound shipping. Initially holding E. Green's economizer patent, with exclusive marketing rights in the United States and Canada, Green Fan was selling industrial fans and rotors to customers in 11 countries by the mid-1970s. Within a decade, however, it closed. Tallix, which sought a move from Peekskill to larger quarters, found the main factory's high ceilings, openness, and industrial equipment a perfect fit.

11

GOV. GEORGE PATAKI, SPEAKING AT DENNING'S POINT, 2003. It may have come as a surprise to some communities along the Hudson that had competed to attract the Rivers and Estuaries Center that Beacon was chosen as the site of the prestigious research facility. However, it did not surprise anyone in Beacon, where locals have long appreciated the breathtaking view from the 64-acre Denning's Point. More than 500 jobs are projected to be created by the $26 million research facility, which is expected to attract 7,000 visitors annually. Its ambitious mission is to develop innovative strategies to protect rivers and estuaries around the world.

SPENCER BARNETT AT DENNING'S POINT RUINS, THE 1970s. In 1988, the New York State Office of Parks and Historic Preservation bought Denning's Point from the Noesting Pin Ticket Company and, thus, fulfilled a dream of the late Spencer Barnett. As city historian, Barnett (inset) was a tireless promoter of the preservation of Denning's Point. His research of the historic peninsula's ties to George Washington and of the history of the Dennings and their magnificent estate, Presqu'ile, was a contributing factor in saving Denning's Point for posterity.

PLAYING CROQUET AT THE DENNING'S MANSION, 1865. By the late 1870s, the elegant lifestyle of the Denning family at Presqu'ile began to disappear. After selling out to Ramsdell enterprises, Emily Denning Van Rensselaer and her daughter Emily remained in their home through the 1880s, though brickyard activities came to surround them. In 1890, when her mother died, Emily left the mansion and the brick workers' families moved in. By the 1920s, the Denning mansion was in ruins.

SWIMMING AT DENNING'S POINT, THE 1920S. Generations of local residents swam in the brackish waters of the Hudson River off Denning's Point, but, for a time, thousands were attracted to the "Coney Island of Dutchess County" for more than just swimming. In the 1920s and 1930s, a popular resort here welcomed large crowds, many of them ferried across the river from Newburgh by motorboat. In addition to swimming and sunbathing, many came to dance the day away to the live music that was featured on Sundays in season.

HORSEPOWER AT THE BRICKYARD, C. 1900. The purchase of Denning's Point for the site of his new brickyard proved to be an excellent business decision for entrepreneur Homer Ramsdell. In the fall of 1880, workmen clearing the east end of the peninsula of brush and trees uncovered immense deposits of clay. On the west side, plentiful clean sand was found. The abundant supply of these key ingredients ensured success for Denning's Point Brick Works for the next 50 years.

THE DENNING'S POINT BRICKYARD, C. 1900. Despite its original bucolic charm, Denning's Point underwent a dramatic transformation due to the brickmaking operations. Working conditions at the brickyards were difficult, to say the least, and prompted, for example, a massive walkout at this and 13 other local yards in 1905. Striking workers demanded a 25¢ raise in their $2 daily rate. The owners, who denounced "the mobs and their methods," conceded a raise of 20¢ per 14-hour workday to end the walkout.

DENNING'S POINT BRICK WORKS, 1925. Bricks with "DPBW" stamped into them can be found everywhere around Beacon. For more than 50 years, those bricks were made at Denning's Point Brick Works, the heyday of which came in the 1920s, when, under the management of David Strickland, 145 men were employed and 300,000 bricks were produced there daily. Strickland is credited with modernizing the plant in 1925 by introducing an electric train (shown) and an electric shovel to make the yard one of the most efficient and profitable along the Hudson. During 1926, the brickyard made an astounding 60 million bricks. By 1939, with the clay banks at Denning's Point deleted, the company moved to its Brockway plant, a few miles north.

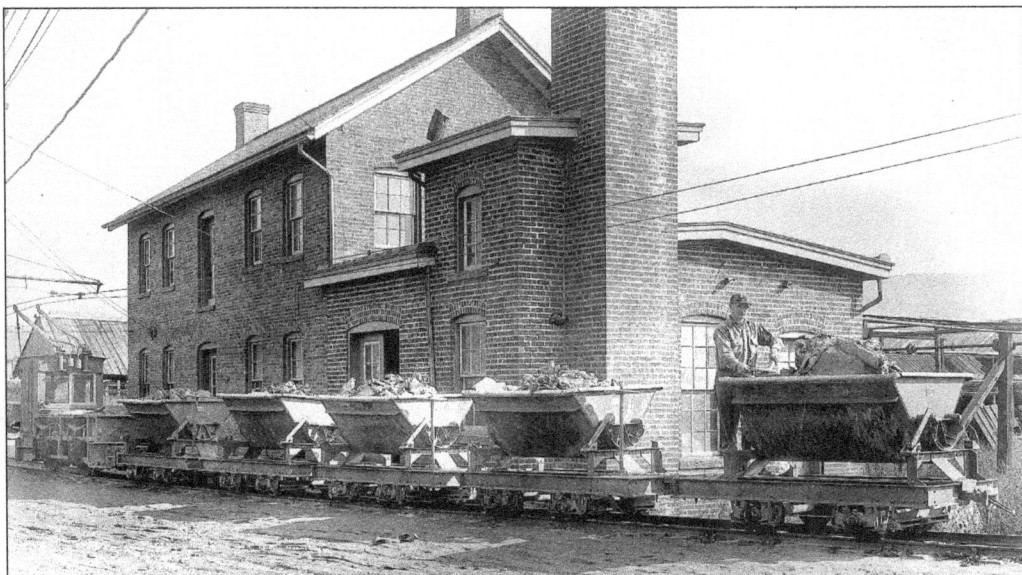

THE EAST END "BEFORE," THE 1980s. After World War II, better roads, automobiles, and economic prosperity sparked the construction of suburban neighborhoods and shopping malls. People no longer needed to live close by in order to work or shop because they could easily drive wherever they wanted to go. By the 1980s, both ends of Beacon's Main Street were in tough shape, as shopkeepers who raised their families above storefronts disappeared one by one. Unused, boarded-up buildings fell victim to neglect, vandalism, and arson; many advocated for demolition.

THE EAST END "AFTER," 1992. The renaissance of Beacon's Main Street can be largely credited to Ron and Ronnie Beth Sauers, who recognized the beauty and potential hidden within the rundown building facades of the East End. They purchased and rehabilitated two buildings and then found a first tenant in antiques dealer Gail Boccia. A gradual domino effect has since revitalized Main Street from end to end. Antique shops, specialty boutiques, eateries, art galleries, and entrepreneurial businesses have breathed new life into great old buildings.

Two

LANDSCAPE

"A view or vista of scenery."

CARS PASSING ON THE INCLINE, C. 1905. By the late 1990s, after a generation of neglect, abandonment, and near oblivion by fire, the Mount Beacon Incline Railway had a reversal of its misfortunes. In 1995 and 1999, Scenic Hudson Land Trust spared the historic site from developers by purchasing two parcels of land on Mount Beacon, including the top and base of the old railway. Contemporaneously, the Mount Beacon Incline Railway Restoration Society was organized to rebuild and restore the railway.

An Outing near the Mount Beacon Monument, c. 1905. The Mount Beacon Incline Railway made it possible for sightseers to experience the rugged beauty of the mountaintop and still wear their finest attire. The facility of the railway and the mountain settings also attracted early filmmakers. In 1909 and 1910, famed director D.W. Griffith made three of his short films, *The Redman's View*, *Fugitive*, and *Song of the Wildwood Flute* (starring a young Mary Pickford as a Native American maiden), on location near the DAR monument.

"Go Devil" Descending Mount Beacon, 1905. With seeming reckless abandon, this nattily dressed man would speed down the mountain, thrilling visitors of the Mount Beacon Incline Railway with his antics. The showman in reality was Edward Sears, the railway's electrician, who rode a one-man sidecar he nicknamed "Go Devil" to get down the mountain quickly. The fearless Sears guided his makeshift vehicle safely for four years until his luck ran out in 1906, when he fell off and never fully recovered.

THE HOWARD COTTAGE ON MOUNT BEACON, 1905. In its heyday, from the early 1900s through the 1940s, the cottage colony on Mount Beacon was a bustling, seasonal community of about 20 families. Frank Howard's cottage, located near the reservoir and farthest from the incline, was one of the first to appear. A string of cottages built on both sides of the half-mile long "Howard's Path" followed. Today, only one inhabitable cabin—owned by Col. Robert Ray—remains among the ruins of cottages along the path.

THE BEAUTIFUL BABY CONTEST ON MOUNT BEACON, 1919. John B. Lodge, manager of the Mount Beacon Incline Railway since 1914, had a keen business sense when it came to promoting his mountain resort. One of the most popular of his special days on the mountain was the Beautiful Baby Contest of September 13, 1919. More than 50 tots and their mothers vied for the $30 in prizes. The twin sons of Harry and Margaret Phillips, Gordon and Kenny (fourth from the left), won first prize: $15 in gold.

RADIO TOWERS AMID SUMMER COTTAGES ON MOUNT BEACON, 1928. On the summit of Mount Beacon, 1,500 feet above sea level, once was located the highest (at the time) broadcasting station in the East: station WOKO, "the Voice from the Clouds." With its two 110-foot-high towers connected by a 190-foot aerial, WOKO made its mountaintop debut in April 1928, broadcasting over a range of 200 miles.

MOUNT SIDE REST HOTEL, 1929. John J. Neville's Mount Side Rest, nestled in a rural setting at the foot of Mount Beacon, was a popular overnight spot for tourists before and after World War II. In the summer of 1939, however, Neville's became the focal point for all local boxing enthusiasts. Light heavyweight champion and Beacon resident Melio Bettina, preparing to defend his crown against Billy Conn, set up his training camp here.

20

BEFORE THE FIRE, 1983. The disastrous late summer fire of 1983, which destroyed the tracks, the two cars, and the powerhouse, left a bleak landscape. Estimates for its reconstruction today run into the millions of dollars. Yet, in 1902, the whole project, from base to summit, cost a little more than $100,000. The money then was raised by the 200 stockholders of the Mount Beacon Incline Railway, four-fifths of whom lived in New Hampshire and Maine.

RIDING THE INCLINE, 1965. Made stable and secure under the ownership of Scenic Hudson Land Trust, with its welfare closely guarded by the Mount Beacon Railway Restoration Society, the railway's future has not looked brighter in decades. Scenic Hudson Land Trust will make the historic site more accessible to the public by building a park at the base of the mountain, with interpretive kiosks and a 300-foot stairway along the old tracks leading to a staging area for a series of trails up the mountain.

21

SKIING ON MOUNT BEACON, 1967–1975. The Dutchess Ski Area offered day and night skiing on 11 trails (2 of them more than a mile in length) and slopes, snowmaking equipment, 2 double-chair lifts, a ski lodge, and a December-through-March season of skiing on the 1,531-foot summit of Mount Beacon. With its proximity to New York City, Dutchess Ski's management hoped to draw up to 1,200 skiers on weekends and thereby help make Beacon a major recreational center.

THE DUTCHESS SKI AREA MELTING AWAY, 1975. Starting in 1970, the Dutchess Ski Area experienced four dry and mild winters in a row. In 1974, the resort's best season in four years, there were only 60 days of skiing compared to a normal season of 90. The energy crisis of that year, which kept metropolitan skiers stuck at home without gasoline to drive north, compounded the financial crisis on the mountain. In 1975, the Dutchess Ski Area went bankrupt. Creditors swarmed in and dismantled the chairlifts.

THE DAR MONUMENT REDEDICATION, JULY 4, 2000. In a grand celebration of patriotism, more than 600 people climbed to the top of Mount Beacon to celebrate the centennial anniversary of the monument erected by the Melzingah Chapter of the Daughters of the American Revolution in 1900. The 27-foot-high monument honors the Revolutionary War patriots who manned a series of signal fires—beacons—that were ordered by the Continental Congress in 1777, and for which the city below was later named.

A BEACON REPLICA, JULY 4, 2000. Costumed reenactors assemble the beacon built and burnt in honor of the monument's centennial anniversary. The 18-foot beacon, constructed of timbers culled from the site of Fort Montgomery and built to Revolutionary War specifications, was burned at 9:00 p.m. Participants in the daylong series of events, which featured Revolutionary War demonstrations and the chance to both sign a copy of the Declaration of Independence and swear an oath of loyalty to the United States, trekked two miles in warm, humid weather to mark the anniversary.

23

A STAGECOACH AT FOUNTAIN SQUARE, C. THE 1880S. Stagecoaches, drawn by teams of bay horses with bells on their collars, were the main means of transport connecting Matteawan Village with the ferry at Fishkill Landing. The fare was 5¢ or 25 rides for $1. The coming of the trolley to the twin villages in 1892 put the stagecoach line out of business. George Mowatt and Stephen Westfall, two drivers for the stagecoach line, quickly found jobs as motormen for the new streetcars.

THE FISHKILL LANDING TRAIN STATION, 1913. With the traffic at its Beacon junction ever increasing, the old New York Central & Hudson River Railroad station no longer met the needs of the railroad's busy Fishkill stop, as it was then named. The New York Central's ambitious three-year (1913–1915) improvement plan for Beacon called for replacing the old station with a modern one, changing the yard's layout, and expanding to a four-track line in place of two.

A NEW RAILROAD BRIDGE, 1914. The new railroad bridge, tying River and Beekman Streets and Newburgh (South) Avenue to the ferry dock, was the final connecting link in the chain of improvements going on at Beacon's waterfront. Before construction began, the village property line ended at the site of the old bridge; the railroad and ferry companies in the past had retained ownership of the street to the docks and station. When the bridge was completed, the railroad turned over its street rights to the new city.

THE STATION UNDER CONSTRUCTION, 1915. The New York Central's expansion of its Beacon holdings entailed a shift to the west, toward the river, for its station house, new tracks, and rail yard. The reclamation of riverfront land required boatloads and carloads of cinder and rock fill to be brought in to raise the level of the track beds. The new train station would be the matching complement to the neighboring ferry terminal, which had just opened the previous year.

BEACON'S NEW WATERFRONT, 1916. The completion of the new "Gateway to Beacon" was the kind of sweeping transformation that literally brought the city's new riverfront image out of the 19th century and into the 20th. Gone were the relics of an older age; the ferry house, train station, old hotels, and factory (swept away by the railroad's expansion) were replaced by modern buildings, wider streets, better bridges, and faster service by trolley, train, and ferry getting to and from Beacon.

THE 1950S WATERFRONT. Through the 1950s, Beacon had a vibrant waterfront, but almost everything in this aerial photograph is today either gone or drastically altered. The ferry house and ferries, the train station and rail yard, the bridge over the tracks, the storage tanks on Long Dock, and the houses along Beekman and River Streets and Wolcott Avenue are all gone. Plans to revive the ferry and to develop the waterfront—including Scenic Hudson Land Trust's proposals to construct an inn and amphitheater—have the potential to bring people back to this area that once served as a vital hub in the community.

"LITTLE MO WON'T GO!" The calls for a bridge between Newburgh and Beacon grew louder after April 10, 1950, when the ferry *Dutchess* got stuck on a mud bank, stranding passengers on the river for hours. For this propensity to get stuck in the mud, the *Dutchess* was tagged with the nickname "Little Mo," after the battleship *Missouri* ("Mighty Mo"), which got stuck in an Atlantic Ocean mud bank around the same time. Schoonmaker's store soon was selling children's T-shirts for 98¢ with a picture of the *Dutchess* and the words "Little Mo Won't Go." "Little Mo has got to go" was the sentiment commonly held thereafter by disgruntled passengers, who had to put up with 21 disruptions of ferry service, including ice in winter, boat disablement, or labor troubles, between 1950 and 1958. Authorization for construction of a new bridge passed the state legislature in 1954.

THE IDEAL FERRY FOR MOTORISTS

Runs from 6.00 A. M. until 11.00 P. M.

From April to November trips are made every half hour, 6.00 A.M. to 10.30 A. M.; every quarter hour, 10.30 A. M. to 7.30 P. M.; every half hour to 11 P. M.

You don't need a Time Table

Only restrictions those of U. S. Steamboat Laws

THE FERRY *ORANGE* WITH RADAR, 1958. Before radar was installed on the *Orange* in 1958, the only tools a ferry captain had to guide the boat to shore through fog and snow were a compass, an alarm clock, and a whistle. The clock told him how far he had gone (the average trip took six or seven minutes), and the whistle, echoing off the hills and tall buildings, signaled how close the boat was to dock. Of course, radar also allowed the technology to avoid sandbars in the river, a problem that plagued the *Dutchess* for years.

FERRIES BATTLING THE ICE, 1961. One of the hardest winters for the ferries (and their passengers) was that of 1934. In February, the ice on the Hudson River was so thick that it damaged the propeller of the *Orange*, causing it to be laid up for repairs in the north slip at Beacon. With ice jams blocking the south slip, the *Dutchess* was forced to dock at the bow of the *Orange*. To reach the shore, cars and passengers warily crossed on heavy planks laid between the boats.

28

THE FERRY *DUTCHESS* REBUILT AFTER THE FIRE, 1962. Early Saturday morning, July 1, 1961, a fire of undetermined origin destroyed the superstructure of the *Dutchess* as it lay in its slip in Newburgh. Once repaired, the Dutchess "probably won't retain her former lines," a New York State Bridge Authority spokesman said. Indeed, it was hardly recognizable. Rebuilt with no upper deck and boxes for pilot houses, its graceful lines were gone. After the fire No Smoking signs were tacked on all three ferries.

THE STATE-OWNED FERRY BEACON, C. 1963. On April 1, 1956, the Newburgh-Beacon Ferry became the property of the New York State Bridge Authority. Homer Ramsdell and his sister Pauline Ramsdell Odell, whose family had privately owned the ferry service for more than 100 years, sold the entire business for $250,000. The bridge authority soon changes the ferries' color from red to green, the state's official color, and the new owner's name was emblazoned in white lettering across the boats' top deck.

29

THE FIRST SPAN OF THE NEWBURGH-BEACON BRIDGE, 1963. The $20 million Newburgh-Beacon Bridge was steely evidence of the expanding interstate highway system that was crisscrossing America by the mid-20th century. The 1.5-mile span allowed Interstate 84 to connect not only Dutchess and Orange Counties, but also Connecticut with Pennsylvania and beyond. Some 25 years in the making, the bridge—estimated to handle 25 years of traffic projections—was dedicated on November 2, 1963, with a grand parade and ceremonial crossing led by Gov. Nelson Rockefeller.

THE SECOND SPAN OF THE BRIDGE, 1980. The $94 million second span of the Newburgh-Beacon Bridge, described as the longest-weathering steel bridge in the world at the time of its construction, was hoisted into place in 1980. As this span was part of the interstate highway system, it was 90 percent financed by the federal government. A promise that the bridge would become toll free once the New York State Bridge Authority's 10 percent of the construction cost was paid off was never kept.

Three

PANORAMA

"A comprehensive picture of a chain of events."

"LET'S PULL TOGETHER," 1913. As early as 1866, meetings between the twin villages were held to form one municipality. Concerns over increased taxes and disagreements over a name kept Mr. Matteawan and Mr. Fishkill Landing (depicted in this banner above Talbot's Saloon) at a figurative, if not literal, distance. A charter committee of 15 recommended a government model copied from the charter of Grand Junction, Colorado. Twice vetoed by successive governors because that city's charter included "western innovations," such as recall and referendum, the charter was modified to remove those elements and finally signed by Gov. William Sulzer on May 15, 1913.

THE MATTEAWAN COMPANY, OLD MATTEAWAN, 1869. Matteawan was a successful factory town for several reasons. The mills that lined the creek harnessed its currents to fuel the manufacture of scores of products. The Dutchess and Columbia Railroad laid tracks through Matteawan in 1866, ensuring the facile transportation of products to all points. Workers, many of them young women seeking jobs from the surrounding countryside, were in plentiful supply. With more than 7,000 residents in 1913, Matteawan had twice the population of Fishkill Landing.

DAVID DAVIS DRY GOODS, OLD MATTEAWAN. The Matteawan Company built the Matteawan Store in 1814 to serve its factory workers. David Davis, who had started as an 18-year-old clerk, bought the concern and changed its name to David Davis Dry Goods when the company failed 25 years later. He was still at the helm in 1877, when the railroad widened the highway near its depot, buying Davis out, and razing the store and several others in the process.

OLD FISHKILL LANDING, C. 1865. Fishkill Landing was a thriving port at a time when the Hudson River was the main artery of transportation for goods and passengers. As early as 1780, a total of 24 vessels were operating out of the landing, as it took "inside 12 hours" to make the trip by sloop from Fishkill Landing to Manhattan. Hotels, transportation connections, and homes all vied for space on the bustling waterfront.

OLD FISHKILL LANDING, THE EARLY 1900S. Laws against speeding applied not only to the automobile. In 1878, Fishkill Landing village officials cracked down on dangerous driving when they passed this ordinance: "No person shall ride on horseback or drive in any street in said village, any horse or horses, mule or mules, at a greater speed than at the rate of six miles per hour."

THE LAST GRADUATING CLASS AT FISHKILL-ON-HUDSON HIGH SCHOOL, 1915. The foundation stone for the new Beacon High School was already in place when the last graduates of Beacon's two old and soon-to-be defunct high schools received their diplomas. These nine members of Fishkill-on-Hudson High School's class of 1915 joined their fellow graduates of Matteawan High School for ceremonies that June at Beacon's Academy of Music theater.

THE ACADEMY STREET SCHOOL (1857–1891). With its students sitting on windowsills and spilling out of the doorway, the Academy Street School had evidently become overcrowded by the 1880s. In 1891, with a new school on South Avenue now open, the old Academy Street School was sold to a manufacturer of products for the baking industry. The Dutchess Tool Company remained in the building for the next 70 years. The adaptive reuse of the old Academy Street School parallels today's proposals for the old Beacon High School.

ROOM NO. 9 AT BEACON HIGH SCHOOL, 1917. On February 14, 1916, the new Beacon High School opened its doors to students from the city's two older high schools. Fishkill-on-Hudson High School had about 90 students to send to that opening session; Matteawan High a few less. To cut costs, school administrators had student desks removed from the old high school and reinstalled in the new. No money was available to build an auditorium or gymnasium at the new school either. Those additions came later, in 1924 and 1925, respectively.

THE BEACON HIGH SCHOOL GRADUATING CLASS, 1925. The class of 1925 had several "firsts" in local graduation annals. It was the first class to hold graduation ceremonies in the school's new (1925) auditorium; William Howes, one of 36 students, was the first African American to graduate from Beacon High School; Edward Todd was the youngest graduate ever at age 14; and Ben Hammond (center), honored for his 36 years as former school board president, probably was the oldest to receive a diploma, albeit an honorary one.

BESKIN'S DEPARTMENT STORE, C. 1900. Three stories high and sporting one of the area's first elevators, Beskin's Department Store was tangible evidence of the rags-to-riches success of Samuel Beskin, a Russian immigrant who arrived speaking little English and who began selling notions on street corners. In time, he came to own a small hotel, brewery, hat factory, and apartment building, in addition to his Bank Square store. He was elected, by a large majority, the second mayor of Beacon in 1915.

A CAMPAIGN SPEECH ON MAIN STREET, 1912. Speaking from the second-story balcony of the Spy Hill Florists, Republican candidate Job E. Hedges had a sympathetic crowd to hear his bid to be elected governor in 1912. Despite strong local support for Hedges, his opponent, Democrat William Sulzer, won the election that November. Sulzer turned out to be an auspicious choice, for on May 16, 1913, he signed into law the Smith Bill, authorizing the incorporation of Matteawan and Fishkill Landing into the city of Beacon.

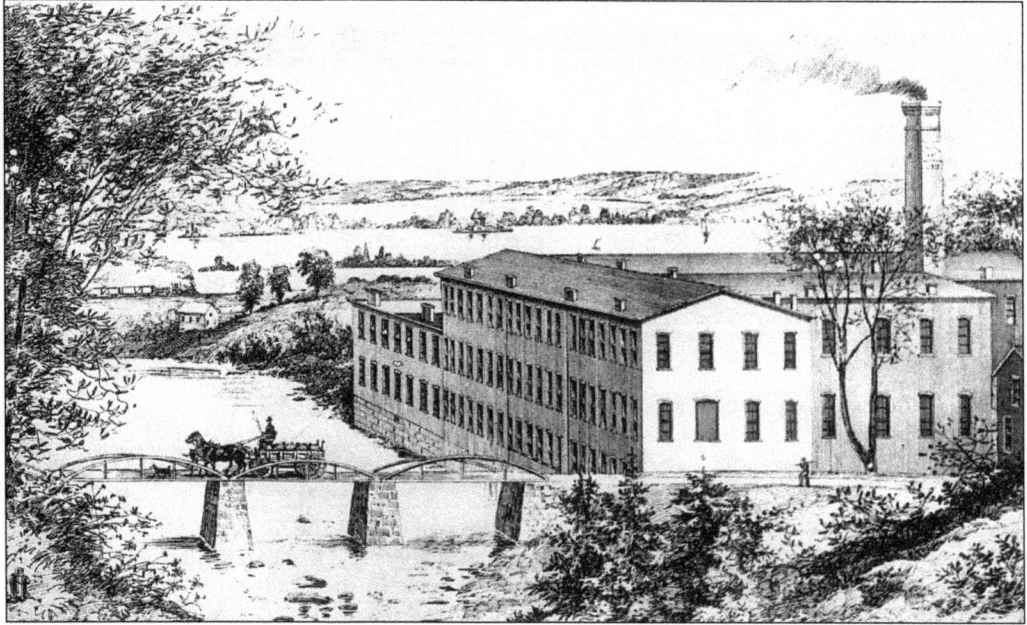

THE TIORONDA BRIDGE, 1879. The 1872 Tioronda Bridge, which crosses the creek from South to Tioronda Avenues, is listed on the National Register of Historic Places as one of only two extant bowstring truss spans in the nation. Its picturesque setting above the rapids of the Fishkill Creek, its connection to the nearby historic hat factory, and its unique original iron trusses have prompted preservationists, including the Beacon Historical Society, to push for its appropriate historical restoration.

BLACKBURN AVENUE CREATED, C. 1907. Streetcars once rode close by the old Green Fuel Economizer company (now the Tallix Foundry) on an upper Main Street much changed from today's. The street changes came about in 1907, when Arthur H. Blackburn, Green Fuel's manager, offered to share the costs of moving the trolley tracks westerly onto a newly created street (thereby expanding his factory's property). Thus, Blackburn Avenue surfaced, and today, a truncated Main Street abruptly ends in a cul-de-sac near the back entrance to the old factory.

37

TROLLEY NO. 5, BEFORE THE FIRE. In the spring of 1928, the Fishkill Electric Railway company burned nine of its obsolete trolley cars in a spectacular cleanup fire at the base of the Mount Beacon Incline. The cars were taking up space in the Main Street barns that were needed for the five new cars due in May. One car, trolley No. 11, did escape the fiery fate. Arthur Hallock bought it, moved it to Fishkill Landing, and converted it into a hot dog and refreshment stand.

"GALLOPING GOOSE" RAIL BUS, 1933. Loss of ridership on the Beacon-to-Pine Plains rail line, which had operated since 1869, led to a decision to replace labor-intensive steam engines with gasoline-driven rail buses. The unattractive bus-on-rails inspired more than a few nicknames, including "Galloping Goose," "Leaping Lena," and the "Toonerville Trolley," but few new passengers. The last paying customer boarded No. 9007 in 1933. Freight trains continued to use the Beacon-Hopewell tracks until the 1990s, the end of the line for a once critical rail connection.

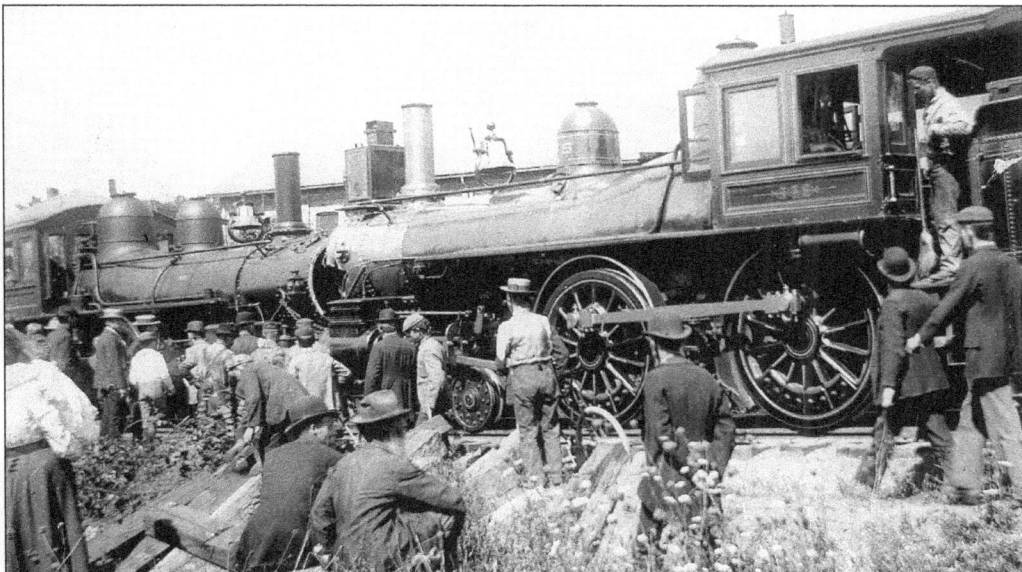

TWO TRAIN WRECKS. The head-on collision of two trains in Matteawan, near the Green Fuel Economizer factory, in 1899 was one of the most spectacular of local railroad mishaps. A more memorable wreck occurred on December 27, 1976, when five freight cars of a ConRail freight train derailed at East Main Street, three of them skidding into the wall of One East Main Street (below). Though the stairwell of the building had to be removed in the aftermath, the remaining portion of the original 1814 stone mill, Beacon's first factory, was salvaged.

THE BYRNESVILLE SALOON, THE 1890S. Though relatively quiet now, the southwest corner of Beacon along the Fishkill Creek was once the bustling hamlet of Byrnesville, which was named for the mill operated by Joseph Byrnes and Robert Newlin and Byrnes's later white-lead factory on the lower reaches of the creek. Factories, a lower landing to the river, a school, and, of course, the ubiquitous saloon provided all the necessities: employment, education, and refreshment.

LYNCH'S BAR. With more than 160 saloons in operation during the 1800s, villagers had no shortage of places to quench their thirst after a long day in the factory. It is little wonder that "Saloon City" received several write-in ballots when residents cast their votes to name their new city. The original charter committee had recommended Melzingah, with Mount Beacon, Tioronda, and Dutchess City collecting a few of the committee's 60 votes; however, the name Beacon won in the popular referendum.

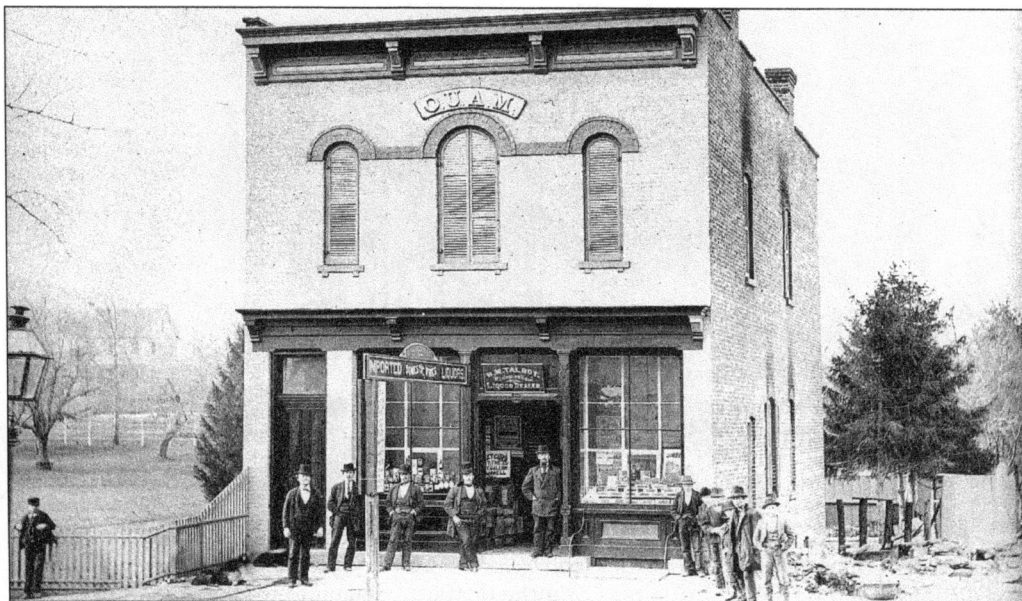

TALBOT'S SALOON, THE 1870s. Talbot's, located at 123 Main Street, was a legal enterprise until 1919, when the Volstead Act put an end to alcohol of any type. Harry Talbot was a man not easily deterred. He converted the front of the bar into a plumbing supply business and simply moved the bar to the back. With liquor imported from Canada and hidden beneath a hinged step on the back stairs, he continued to quench the thirst of loyal patrons until Prohibition was lifted.

THE LAST CIGAR STORE INDIAN IN BEACON, 1928. Winfield Aston, a tobacconist on Main Street since 1884, held the distinction of having the second-oldest business in Beacon. His tiny store at 286 Main Street had on its sidewalk an advertising icon even older than Aston himself. It was a life-sized wooden Indian maiden, one of the last cigar store Indians in the Hudson Valley at the time. The maiden was, up until Aston's death in 1938, the most recognizable folk art fixture on Main Street.

THE PEATTIE BLOCK, 1905. Like other roadways, the west end of early Main Street was not a paved surface. Winter snow, spring rain, and the dry dust of summer made travel difficult and dirty. In 1850, the Fishkill Plank Road Company launched plans to construct a plank road from Fishkill Landing to Stormville. Ten feet wide and made of spruce timbers, the roadway was financed by tollbooths with a 6¢ fee per team. The cycle of frost and flood proved too much for the planks, which lasted just a few years before angry patrons destroyed the tollbooths.

"OLD" 141 MAIN STREET. Twenty years after the twin villages merged to form a new city, there was still plenty of confusion over address numbering on streets that ran in an east–west direction. In 1932, the system was revamped, with numbers running consecutively on streets such as Main, Rombout, and Verplanck. For example, the Howland Library (current Howland Center) became No. 477 after years as No. 553. Today, it is the then-and-now numbers that confuse property owners and researchers using old maps, photographs, documents, or deeds.

NATE BERNSTEIN, 1936. The Bernstein family was a Main Street fixture for decades. Father Ausher Bernstein opened his first store in Fishkill Landing *c.* 1915 and 10 years later moved it to larger quarters at 133–135 Main Street. His son Nathan took over the family business in 1935, and his brother Max sold toys from his own East End emporium. Notably, Max Bernstein also filmed home movies of many Beacon soldiers departing for the front in World War II.

MANNING'S STORE, C. 1935. Hundreds of Beacon residents turned out to view the newfangled contraption on display at Ralph A. Manning's 500 Main Street store, which had recently switched from selling auto parts to selling electronics. RCA Victor's "Modern Marvel" promised to bring "sight and sound to your very living room." Every Tuesday through Friday, Manning's store broadcast New York City television programs from 12:00 p.m. until 1:00 p.m. and from 8:30 p.m. until 9:30 p.m., courtesy of a giant antenna on the roof.

43

THE M.H. FISHMAN DEPARTMENT STORE OPENING, JUNE 17, 1949. Deemed the most modernistic building in Beacon upon its opening in 1949, Fishman's in Beacon was the 41st store in the company's chain. The store, with its solid maple paneling and mirrored columns, featured 60 departments for shopping, including a fountain and luncheonette. By the mid-1970s, like Beacon's other two big department stores, Fishman's had closed, soon to become the new home of the Howland Public Library.

BOCCIA'S MARKET, 1937. An Italian immigrant who arrived in America in 1918, Gaetano Boccia and his wife opened their store in 1924, selling meats, vegetables, and groceries to the city's hungry factory workers. A Main Street fixture for 45 years, Boccia's market at the corner of North Street also financed the opportunities only a new world could afford first-generation citizens. The Boccias, described by their son as "great believers in education" sent eight children to college, all of whom became professionals in fields such as law, teaching, and engineering.

A SUPERMARKET SHOPPING FRENZY, 1959. After a five-week nationwide strike of its chain stores, the A & P supermarket on Fishkill Avenue had all 10 of its checkout counters operating to serve the large crowd of returning customers on July 30, 1959. The addition of two big supermarkets (the Empire and the A & P) to Beacon during the 1950s foreboded the end of the small, neighborhood market. In the coming decades, many of Beacon's mom-and-pop stores closed, driven out of business by the bigger competition.

45

BROWNIE SCOUTS IN A MEMORIAL DAY PARADE, 1968. In 1921, the first Girl Scout troop in Dutchess County was organized in Beacon. Then called the Beacon Council, the local group was started by Annie Gurnee, who in those early years had met personally with Juliette Low, the founder of the Girl Scouts movement. That first handful of scouts, Beacon Troop No. 1—the Mountain Laurel troop—was led by Frances Haire. By 1961, Beacon had 1,000 Girl Scouts in 75 troops.

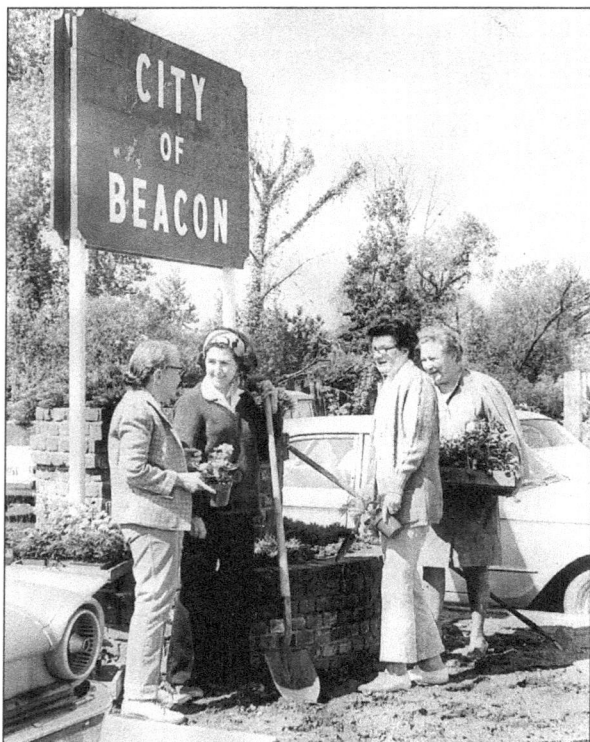

WELCOME TO BEACON, 1973. Tioronda Garden Club members Mary Best, Betty Barnett, Nell Erts, and Vivian Bolton decorate Beacon's new welcome sign at the train station. The club's roots reach back to the Fishkill Landing and Matteawan Plant, Flower, and Fruit Guild, formed in 1900 to ship fresh flowers to the mission houses and tenements of New York City. Although the guild ebbed away during World War I, many of its members met to form the Tioronda Garden Club in 1929. The club has forever since worked to beautify the city, and in 2003, it dedicated Beacon's Patriot Garden on Verplanck Avenue.

Four

VIGNETTES

"Individual stories."

FINISHING HATS, 1952. Kartiganer's, which had moved into the old Dutchess Hat Works on lower Main Street in 1936, was on shaky legs by the mid-1950s, as the last of the big hat shop employers left in Beacon, once the hat-making capital of the state. A few years earlier, layoffs to the 200 workers at the Merrimac Hat Company (located in Tompkins's other old factory, the Tioronda Hat Shop) forewarned of the industry's decline in the city. Merrimac Hat Company's manager, J. Gordon Tompkins, put the blame on America's trend toward "hatlessness."

TIORONDA, C. 1970. A first-time visitor arriving at the southern entrance to Beacon will discover the last vestiges of the city's great estates in coming upon the grounds of Tioronda, built by Joseph and Eliza Howland during the Civil War. The main house was designed by Frederick Clarke Withers; his use of polychromed patterns of brick and stone was an innovation in American Picturesque Gothic. The estate's grounds, while now largely overgrown, were originally landscaped by neighbor Henry Winthrop Sargent.

CRAIG HOUSE HOSPITAL, C. 1970. The estate was sold in 1915 to Dr. C. Jonathan Slocum, who rechristened it Craig House in tribute to a progressive psychiatric facility in Scotland. Slocum "rapidly built the finest psychiatric hospital in the country and probably the world during the 35 years he managed it, until his death in 1950," according to his son, who administered Craig House from the time of his father's death until 1984. Private rooms and secluded cottage living were only part of the appeal.

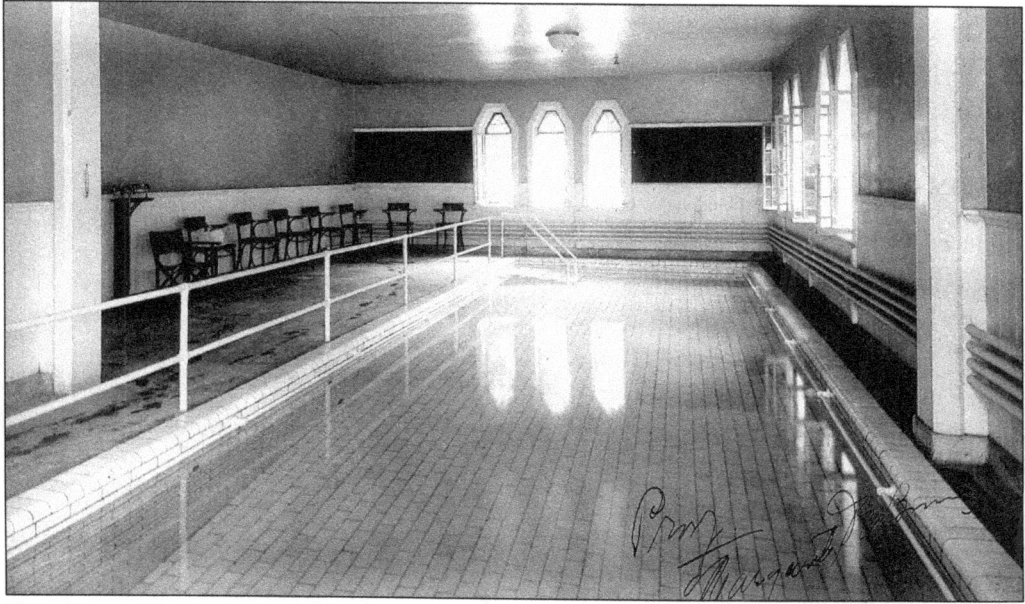

THE CRAIG HOUSE POOL. The Slocums' groundbreaking treatment methods made the hospital an instant success, and within six years, the facility expanded from 100 to 380 acres, with 25 outbuildings and numerous amenities available to its well-to-do patients, including an indoor swimming pool, a private golf course, horseback riding, and an arts and crafts building. Some of the most prominent families in America sent loved ones to Craig House to recuperate from mental illnesses and addictions. While individual psychotherapy remained at the core of treatment, options came to also include electroconvulsive therapy and hypnotherapy.

GRAPE VINEYARDS ON THE GROUNDS OF CRAIG HOUSE. As innovative as its treatment options and as lavish as its lifestyle and grounds once were, times changed, and the Craig House eventually began to decline. Patients who lived in distant regions of the country were referred to closer, newer psychiatric facilities. By the 1990s, managed healthcare, which reduced the reimbursement rates for treatment of the mentally ill, severely impacted the hospital's profitability. On the day of its closing in 2000, fewer than 25 patients were being treated.

A WEST VIEW OF THE SARGENT MANSION, 1930. Horticulturist Henry Winthrop Sargent's estate, Wodenethe, with its artistic gardens and exotic trees, was called "the most beautiful 20 acres in America" by *Country Life in America* magazine in 1912. Sargent's home was the ornate complement to his gardens. After a remodel by noted architect Calvert Vaux, the mansion had three stories with 48 rooms, including a large conservatory that held wintered-over plants and trees from a Mediterranean garden. In its century-long existence, Wodenethe had only two owners, but two very different uses.

SARGENT'S GARDEN GATE, C. 1875. A disciple of Andrew Jackson Downing, Sargent turned his estate into what one expert called "the finest specimen of modern landscape gardening in America." The two Sargents, father and son (Henry Winthrop and Winthrop Henry), are shown potting plants. Nearby, their ornamental gate, composed of rakes, scythes, hoes, and a shovel, is a whimsical testament to a man who became the first American inducted into London's Royal Horticultural Society.

SARGENT'S WODENETHE AS A PATIENTS' HOME, 1919. The death of Aimee Sargent, the last member of Henry Sargent's family in Beacon, necessitated the sale of Wodenethe. In 1919, Dr. Clarence J. Slocum, head of Craig House, bought the Sargent estate, house, grounds, and cottages, for use as an annex to his sanitarium at Tioronda. The sale of the grand estate to become a psychiatric hospital was in keeping with the last wishes of Aimee Sargent, who wanted Wodenethe to someday be "a benefit to the sick and suffering."

WODENETHE BURNED AND RAZED, 1954. Wodenethe was burned to the ground, with Beacon Engine Company standing by, on December 11, 1954. It had been used as a residents' home for Craig House sanitarium since 1925. In 1955, the estate was divided sold as parcels for the new Wodenethe Drive development. Several extant gardening specimens are the only reminders of this once magnificent Hudson River Valley estate.

PRESENTATION CONVENT AND HIDDENBROOKE ESTATE. Originally constructed as a home for notable resident Chancellor Kent, the fine structure above once overlooked the Hudson River from its perch below today's Monell Place. In 1890, the 15-acre estate was purchased by the Sisters of the Presentation, who were seeking a respite from the heat of New York City's summers. They enjoyed the property for 30 years. In 1920, an ember from a passing train sparked a grass fire that consumed the convent, leaving behind only a few chapel benches and two statues. J. Noah Slee built Hiddenbrooke, the Tudor-style mansion below, on a more-than-200-acre parcel at the foot of the mountain for his wife Mary and their children in 1913. Upon divorcing Mary nine years later, Slee married noted birth-control advocate Margaret Sanger, and the property was sold to the Ursuline Sisters. The religious order used the home as a convent and attached a brick chapel to its northern end. Only that chapel could be salvaged after a disastrous nighttime fire razed the main building in 1972.

CARETAKER'S DAUGHTERS AT EDGE HILL, C. 1905. During the Civil War, Smith T. Van Buren, former Pres. Martin Van Buren's only living son, moved to Matteawan and lived in a large house called Edge Hill, located on what is today the Sargent School property and facing Knevels Avenue. Van Buren, together with his wife, four daughters, and son (and a caretaker's family, photographed here), lived at Edge Hill for 12 years until his death in 1876. He is buried in St. Luke's Cemetery.

THE DE LA MONTAGNIE COTTAGE, C. 1864. Clearly, the twin villages were home to some of the finest of the great Hudson River Valley estates, often credited to some of the most foremost architects of the period. This home on South Avenue was designed by Calvert Vaux as a small country cottage for Dr. John de la Montagnie. Now altered and enlarged, the home was originally built into a hollow to take full advantage of its mountain and river views. Vaux's biographer was called it "one of the finest embodiments of the mood of rural intimacy in Vaux's early career."

53

SEWELL'S CARRIAGE WORKS, 1887. Sewell's was one of three post–Civil War carriage and sleigh manufacturers operating in Beacon. In 1887, brothers Samuel and John Sewell moved into their three-story building at today's 207 Main Street, where their arched passageway remains visible. The ground floor housed the blacksmith, woodworking shop, and showroom; the second was used for trimming and painting; housing tenements were located on the top floor.

FURNITURE MADE AT GROVEVILLE MILLS, C. 1950. The prodigious list of raw materials needed yearly at Lewittes and Sons, furniture manufacturers in Beacon from 1934 until 1962, included 75,000 pounds of tacks, 150 carloads of lumber, 400,000 yards of fabric, and another 75,000 pounds of duck and goose down. About 300 workers fashioned the tons of feathers, cotton, and mahogany into some 50,000 units of upholstered furniture, most sold in the department stores of New York and other large cities.

DUTCHESS TOOL WORKS CONVERSION, 1944. Some of Beacon's most capable machinists worked at Dutchess Tool before the war, when the company was manufacturing bakery equipment and employing some 60 men. With the arrival of World War II, the company and its competent work force smoothly switched production gears from its domestic bakery line to vital maritime defense work. Between 500 and 600 men worked three shifts seven days a week to turn out ship telemotors, deck machinery, and bakery equipment for galleys on *Liberty* and *Victory* cargo ships. On July 22, 1944, Dutchess Tool Works received the U.S. Maritime Commission's M award in recognition of outstanding achievement in the commission's shipbuilding program.

DUTCHESS TOOL CO., INC.
OF BEACON, N.Y.
GOES TO WAR

1941

BAKING

MACHINERY

1943

BAKING
MACHINERY
—
BEACON
TELEMOTORS

EVERY LIBERTY SHIP IS STEERED BY A
BEACON TELEMOTOR
MANUFACTURERS OF DECK MACHINERY AND
BAKING EQUIPMENT

DUTCHESS TOOL CO., INC.
BEACON, N.Y.

BACK THE ATTACK WITH WAR BONDS

APRIL, 1944   *Shipmate — April 1944*   61
                     advertisment discontinued
                     May 17th du

MARILYN AND DOUG FISHER WITH BOOKIE BLOX, C. 1927. Charles Fisher's Toy Krofters manufactured fine children's toys on the upper floors of the old Jackson Carriage Works building on Main Street in the 1920s. Among the company's best-sellers were dollhouses and wooden toys such as Bookie Blox, which Fisher's children demonstrate here in the family's South Avenue living room. However, the Great Depression devastated the toy industry, and the Beacon company was soon forced out of business; the Fishers' home and its contents were sold at auction in the bankruptcy that followed.

A SWIFT BILL OF GOODS, 1872. Henry Sargent, landscape artist and summer resident of Matteawan, returned from England one year with a contraption designed to cut grass. When asked to complete some repairs to the device, Horatio N. Swift made so many improvements that his new design bested the original. Soon, 35 hands were needed to turn out nearly 3,000 machines a year from Swift's Roundhouse factory on the Fishkill Creek. Failing to patent his invention, however, Swift never received credit, while one of his workers, Thomas Coldwell, started his own business in Newburgh and dominated the market well into the 20th century.

CHIARELLA FIREWORKS, THE 1920S.
Joseph Chiarella built his factory at the
top of Beacon's East Main Street, in a
remote field at the foot of Mount Beacon.
The location turned out to be not quite
remote enough, as on an early morning
in September 1924, fireworks went off
unexpectedly, killing a worker, scaring
half of Beacon to death, and causing
an estimated $50,000 in damages to
surrounding homes. Operations were moved
to Chelsea in the aftermath.

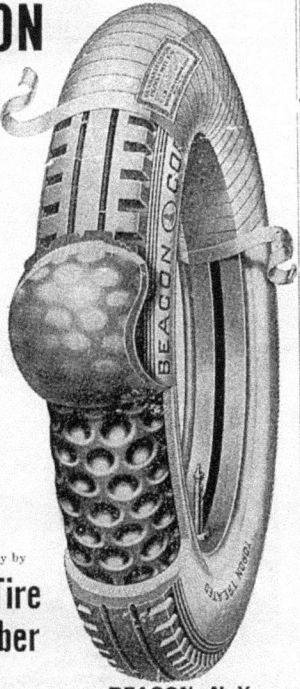

BEACON TIRE AND RUBBER, THE 1920S. In
the days of automobile legend, of frequent
blowouts and the inevitable flat tire, along
came a Beacon rubber product with a guarantee
of 15,000 miles, a remarkably high standard
for its day. The tires were advertised to be
priced "no higher than other quality tires."
The Beacon cords, with their dimple, leakproof
tubes, were manufactured at Beacon Tire and
Rubber Corporation's 204 River Street factory.

FISHKILL TELEPHONE CO.

1. The instruments connected with the Exchange are exclusively for the use of subscribers, and OTHERS MUST NOT BE PERMITTED TO USE THEM for sending business messages, except that with the consent of the lessee the instrument may be used to call a Physician, or send news of general interest to the Local Papers for publication, provided that the parties to whom the messages are sent are subscribers to the Exchange.

2. Excepting inquiries at the Post Office, messages must not be sent to the Central Office to be delivered personally by the operatives.

3. The Central Office will be open from 6 A. M. to 9 P. M.—Sundays from 9 to 10 A. M. and 5 to 6 P. M.

SUBSCRIBERS.

No. of Annunciator.		Magneto Signal.	No. of Annunciator.		Magneto Signal.
8	Alden, H. A.	4	23	Matteawan Depot,	
19	Brundage & Place,		24	Member & Sons, J. E.	
23	Bevier, H. B.		3	New York Rubber Co.	
25	Brundage, Chas. W.		7	Peattie Brothers,	
13	Cordwell, S. A.		11	Place, John	
23	Dutchess Hat Works,	3	11	Slack, Henry	
18	First National Bank,		12	Smith, S. G. & J. T. Land'g	2
20	Fishkill L. Machine W'ks.		12	Smith, S. G. & J. T. Matt'n	3
13	Journal Office,		12	Smith, J. T.	4
20	Kimball, C. L.		19	Sloat, John L.	
25	Kitteredge, W. M.		16	Stotesbury Bros. & Co.	
7	Mechanics Savings Bank,		21	Schenck, J. P.	
9	Mapes, S.		24	Standard Office,	
10	Mt. Gulian House,		22	Tompkins, Lewis	4
15	Macneil, C. C.		22	Tompkins, E. L.	6
16	McDowell, John		22	Tioronda Hat Works,	2
17	Matteawan M'f'g Co.	3	14	Wolcott & Kent,	2
17	Mase, W. H.	4	14	Wolcott, Charles M.	4
21	Moore, W. H.				

THE FIRST TELEPHONE DIRECTORY, 1880. A newfangled device arrived in the twin villages in April 1880: the telephone. Service was limited in use to the 37 official subscribers with two exceptions: others, with permission, could call a physician or provide "news of general interest to the local paper." Operators assisted all callers until 1961, although the New York Telephone Company had promised direct-dialing service to the Beacon public as early as 1930.

THE NEW TELEPHONE BUILDING, SOUTH BRETT AND MAIN STREETS, 1907. On a Saturday evening in October 1907, the switchboard lights of the Hudson River Telephone Company lit up for the first time as operators relayed calls about town from their handsome new office building on Main Street in Fishkill Landing. Embedded with all of the latest technology, it also included special booths set up on the first floor for what the company called the "transient users of the service," for in reality, the majority of people were still not connected at home. These were the first public pay telephones in Beacon.

FACTORIES ALONG THE FISHKILL CREEK, 1948. The old Matteawan mills of the early 19th century sprouted up beside the rapids and falling waters of the Fishkill Creek. Along its two-mile course through town, from Groveville to Tioronda, six dams were built to harness the Fishkill for the earliest manufacturers. This aerial view of the East Main Street factories, Braendly Dye Works and the Bobrich, focuses on the center of the old Matteawan mills district, first begun in 1814.

THE DUTCHESS HAT WORKS.

TWO TOP HAT SHOPS IN BEACON, 1913. The Matteawan Manufacturing Company, begun in 1864, and the Dutchess Hat Works, begun in 1874, were the two hat factories in the vanguard of Beacon's rise to the top of hat-manufacturing cities in the Northeast (second only to Danbury, Connecticut). In 1913, Matteawan Manufacturing, on East Main Street, made wool and felt hats and employed 332 men and 70 women. Dutchess Hat, on lower Main and Bank Streets, manufactured felt hats and employed 148 men and 68 women.

59

FERRY AND BEEKMAN STREETS IN A VIEW LOOKING EAST, 1965. It was the most controversial event ever to happen to Beacon, and it most assuredly changed the face of the city more than anything else before or since. Proponents said it was the only way to revitalize the city; opponents feared for property values, relocation impacts, and loss of historic building stock. Urban renewal, a federal program launched in the 1960s to revitalize blighted downtowns, removed blocks of historic streetscapes to replace them with low- and moderate-income housing, highways, and commercial-industrial buildings.

FERRY AND BEEKMAN STREETS IN A VIEW LOOKING WEST, 1965. Although more than 2,300 local signatures once appeared on a petition to halt the federal program and the city council itself voted three to two to suspend participation, urban renewal moved forward. A bipartisan citizens committee endorsed Phase I of the plan in 1966, recommending that a highway be constructed to connect the Newburgh-Beacon Bridge to Route 9D south of the city (a project that took nearly 20 years to achieve). Additional plans included creation of the Henry Street parking lots; destruction of the Brandfield Building, opposite the post office; and creation of both the Liberty Street Garden Apartments and a 35-acre industrial park on Route 52. Streets were paved and landscaped, and a secondary sewage treatment plant was built.

URBAN RENEWAL DESTRUCTION, 1965. Urban renewal realigned streets, removing, for example, the lower end of Main Street and leaving the waterfront disconnected from the business district. It claimed approximately 150 homes and forever changed the look and feel of many neighborhoods. Displaced families received as much as $5,000 above the market value of their homes and $200 toward moving expenses; many relocated to the more than 500 new housing units that were constructed. Some monies were also allocated to help finance rehabilitation of sound, though run-down, properties through low-interest loans. Several parks were also built.

THE FIRST TENANT IN FORRESTAL HEIGHTS GARDEN APARTMENTS, 1970. The first urban renewal project to reach completion was Forrestal Heights, a high-rise with 125 apartments for the elderly and 50 more for families. The Unity Interfaith Housing Corporation of Beacon, a group including ministers from various churches, spearheaded the construction of 124 garden apartments on five acres on South Avenue. The first tenant was Theresa Bugg, shown with, from left to right, Mayor Bob Cahill and Beacon Housing Authority officials Vincent Romanelli and Earle Robinson. By 1973, on an investment of $100,000, Beacon had obtained $20 million in federal funds and urban renewal had left its irreversible imprint on the city.

TAKING THE BANK OUT OF BANK SQUARE, 1957. Sgt. George Garrison, with submachine gun in hand, and other Beacon police officers keep guard as safety deposit boxes are removed from the old Fishkill National Bank building. Established as the First National Bank of Fishkill Landing, Beacon's oldest bank had been a fixture on Bank Square for nearly 100 years. On July 29, 1957, with its new Main Street branch opening a few blocks away, Fishkill National was closing shop at 1 South Avenue forever.

THE CITY DUMP ON FIRE, THE 1960S. This plume of smoke was no cause for alarm: the Beacon city dump was set ablaze virtually every Saturday throughout the 1950s and 1960s in order to dispose of residents' accumulated garbage. The dump, created in the 1930s when eight barges were sunk to create the perimeter of the peninsula at the then foot of Main Street, was filled to capacity by 1964. In June, the city's new incinerator went on line. A grass-roots movement to create Riverfront Park resulted in its official dedication at the 1980 Strawberry Festival.

MAIN STREET, THE 1970S. The look of Main Street has changed in many ways. Both ends have literally been removed: the western terminus eliminated during urban renewal and the eastern end converted to a cul-de-sac at the back gate to the Tallix Art Foundry. Planners also once instituted a policy to convert either end of the remaining Main Street into residential apartments, leaving only the central portion as a business district. The current renaissance has reclaimed those storefronts and largely converted them back to commercial use.

"THE GEM OF BEACON" GETTING A NEW ROOF, 1999. The aging slate roof of the Howland Cultural Center had to be replaced. How could its members hope to raise the $50,000 needed to receive a matching grant from the state's Department of Parks, Recreation, and Historic Preservation? The children of Sargent, Forrestal, South Avenue, and Glenham Elementary Schools set an example for the rest of the community by collecting $7,000 in pennies for the roof fund. In 1999, the Howland Center had a new black Canadian slate roof.

THE REDEDICATION OF THE CIVIL WAR STATUE, 1989. Former Congressman Hamilton Fish Sr. was the keynote speaker at June 1989 ceremonies to rededicate Beacon's monument to Civil War soldiers. The monument had been placed in the Fairview Cemetery in 1903 but was toppled by vandals sometime in the 1970s. The Beacon Historical Society, with the assistance of local artisan Luigi DeDominicis, returned the statue to its base and fenced off the surrounding veterans' burial plot before rededicating the statue in a ceremony that attracted hundreds.

THE DEDICATION OF THE WASHINGTON BUST, SEPTEMBER 5, 1999. As part of a nationwide celebration sponsored by Mount Vernon to mark the bicentennial of George Washington's death, the Melzingah Chapter of the Daughters of the American Revolution gave Beacon a bronze bust of the first president. Beacon's first public monument since the Hebe statue had been dedicated for the Hudson-Fulton celebration of 1909, it was erected at Teller and Wolcott Avenues to recall Washington's visits to the nearby Madam Brett Homestead during the Revolutionary War.

Five

SKETCHES

"A quick drawing; a brief composition."

A HORSE AND SLEIGH, C. 1900. This winter snow scene, taken at the corner of Jackson and Grove Streets, is probably by Beacon amateur photographer Charles Getler. In years past, Grove Street (where the Getler family resided) was known as Getler's Hill. A hundred years ago, a horse and sleigh out for a winter day's ride after a storm was a common sight on many streets. Even Main Street was not routinely plowed until the 1920s.

THE MELZINGAH DAM FLOOD, JULY 14, 1897. Twenty-two consecutive days of rain forced both dams of the Melzingah Reservoir to burst sometime after midnight and unleashed a river of water that plunged down the mountainside and through the brickyard below. Buildings were crushed and railroad tracks washed away. Those who heard the roar of the deluge in time managed to escape, but seven people, including three children, were lost in the 12 million gallons of rushing waters. Among the dead was Mary Conroy, the 30-year-old wife of the brickyard's engineer, who had somehow managed to miraculously escape death during the great Johnstown flood, only to lose her life here. A jury found the Fishkill and Matteawan Water Company responsible for the tragedy, in that it failed to maintain the dams with adequate spillways. Concrete dams were built to replace the original structures, and the city post-tensioned those facilities in 1993 to ensure a reliable water supply for at least another century.

A DOUBLE FUNERAL ON DEWINDT STREET, 1912. A young boy's death, by accident or disease, was not an uncommon occurrence here in 1912. But when two brothers, Thomas and Victor Ferry, were struck and killed by lightning while picking cherries at their home on Dewindt Street, their funeral warranted special attention. Fellow classmates carried the coffins from the boys' house to two white, horse-drawn hearses, which then carried them to services at St. John's Church.

THE BLIZZARD OF 1888. Everyone who owned a horse turned out to clear the roads following the Blizzard of 1888's record snowfall. With drifts of 3 to 11 feet, only horses and sleighs could break a path after the March 12 storm. Using double teams, Weston's stagecoach line was the first to pack down the snow on Main Street. Shopkeepers were forced to tunnel through the snow that was pushed to the sidewalks. Ben Hammond recalled the silence after the storm: "Not a train whistle to be heard," he wrote in his diary, "all the trains were stopped."

THE BLIZZARD OF 1902. A two-day snowfall of nearly three feet paralyzed the villages in February 1902. Barn roofs collapsed under the weight of the accumulation and, according to local press accounts, "dealers in snow shovels did a rushing business and could have sold many more if they had them to sell." All along Main Street, the snow was piled high to be carted away by hand and dumped in vacant lots. "This gave work to many men who were glad of the opportunity to earn a few dollars," the *Fishkill Standard* reported.

THE GREAT FLOOD OF MARCH 1, 1902. A night of torrential rain melted winter snow, sending cakes of ice and pieces of timber rushing down the Fishkill. Locals could not recall anything quite like the torrent that closed bridges over the creek, submerged the electric plant, and washed out railroad tracks. Residents deserted their homes along the creek, taking only what valuables they could carry. Among them was John Bradley, who nearly drowned trying to rescue the liquor from his Spring Valley Street saloon; onlookers pulled him ashore with a rope.

THE CEMETERY OF CONVICTS, 1985. At the edge of a stand of tall evergreens not far from Beacon's new high school lies the state-owned cemetery wherein hundreds of unknown men and women are buried. Between the opening of the Matteawan State Hospital (then the Asylum for the Criminally Insane) in 1892, its closing in 1977, and its transformation into Fishkill Correctional Facility, about 1,800 inmates and patients were buried in this remote corner of the prison's grounds. Today, only numbered stones mark the graves of these unfortunates.

St. Joachim's Church, 1910. Up to the mid-19th century, the village of Matteawan's burgeoning Catholic community held Mass only in makeshift churches, even in a converted barn on Fishkill Avenue. In 1853, a parish church was established a stone's throw away from the neighboring Presbyterian church (already established there for 20 years) on Leonard Street. The new St. Joachim's Church was formally dedicated on August 18, 1861, the feast day of its patron saint.

The Reformed Church of Beacon, 1910. Organized as a congregation in 1813 as an offshoot of the historic Reformed Church of Fishkill, the current church building was designed by Frederick Clarke Withers and dedicated in 1861. Its spire was added in 1880. Of historic note was the interment of Col. William Few in the church's graveyard. He signed the U.S. Constitution as a delegate from Georgia. While never a local resident, he died while visiting his daughter in Fishkill Landing. His remains were removed to Georgia in 1973 by then Gov. Jimmy Carter.

Dutch Reformed Church, Fishkill Landing, N. Y.

ST. LUKE'S CHURCH. Two of Beacon's most prominent citizens, Charles Wolcott and Henry E. Davies, donated the land on which to build St. Luke's Church (after expansion of the railroad forced the congregation of St. Anna's on Main Street to seek a new home). A third notable resident, Henry Winthrop Sargent, landscaped the grounds of the church, which had been designed by Frederick Clarke Withers. The cornerstone of the church was laid on October 17, 1868, in a period of great postwar rebuilding.

ST. ANDREW'S CHURCH. When the Episcopalians of Fishkill Landing decided that the trip to Matteawan to attend services at St. Luke's was simply too great, they built their own church on South Avenue. Complete with windows designed by Louis Comfort Tiffany, St. Andrew's was dedicated in 1900. By the early 1950s, the church had taken a leadership role in improving race relations in the city. A playground was built to involve neighborhood youth, and the Martin Luther King Cultural Center was established in an adjoining building.

71

THE DEDICATION OF THE CHURCH OF THE NAZARENE, 1924. More than 350 members of the Groveville Park Association marched in a parade from their Groveville campground to dedicate the new Nazarene Church on Teller Avenue and Henry Street on July 19, 1924. The Nazarenes of that era were perhaps best remembered as being the local hosts to huge camp-rally meetings in Groveville Park, where they held fervid services during the summer. The Red Men later purchased the church building and used it for their meeting hall.

GROVEVILLE COTTAGES, C. 1915. In the 1890s, Groveville Park, located near the outskirts of the city between the Fishkill Creek and upper Washington Avenue, was a popular amusement park and the last-stop destination of the local streetcar. By the early 1900s, the rides and trolleys were gone due to a lack of interest and the park had become home to a cottage colony of four-room bungalows, available for rent to the Nazarenes and summer vacationers. Today, many of these cottages survive in a variety of forms, having been incorporated into traditional family homes.

THE BEACON THEATRE, 1950. On August 7, 1934, the date that owner Max Ginsberg opened the new Beacon Theatre, excitement was in the air as hundreds lined up to see Marion Davies and Gary Cooper star in the film *Operator 13*. The atmosphere of the new theater, built on the site of the old Dibble Opera House, was that of posh elegance, red velour draperies, soft carpets, and walls of Italian marble. Ticket prices that opening night were 40¢ for adults, 15¢ for children.

THE ROOSEVELT THEATRE LOBBY, 1950. In the lobby of the Roosevelt Theatre are movie posters of Jane Powell, starring in *Two Weeks with Love,* and Marshall Heroy (right), ready to take tickets. The Roosevelt Theatre in 1950 was one of two theaters on Main Street, both owned by Max and Ben Ginsberg. When it opened in 1934, the Roosevelt had stiff competition from three other movie houses: the Beacon, the Apollo, and the Paragon. Beacon was entertained for the next 35 years.

THE SOUTHERN DUTCHESS COUNTRY CLUB, THE EARLY 1900S. Twelve of Fishkill Landing's most prominent citizens, among them Ralph Tompkins, Weldon Weston, Arthur Blackburn, and Henry Montgomery, founded the Southern Dutchess Country Club in November 1901. Tompkins had acquired the club's first 50 acres, which included the historic Johannes Coerte Van Voorhis "Stone Cot" farmhouse. Almost immediately, a covered porch was erected on the north side and a bowling alley added to the south. In time, nearly 65 acres were added to the club's expansive grounds.

A CIVIL WAR CANNON ON THE GREEN, C. THE 1920S. As they march down Beekman Street on their way to catch the ferry to Newburgh, members of Usifer's City Band pass a small island in the road that holds Beacon's Civil War cannon. Manufactured during the war at Beacon's Fishkill Landing Machine company, the cannon was given to the city by the local chapter of the Grand Army of the Republic. A few years later, the gun was removed from this spot and placed behind the Casino on Mount Beacon.

CITY BOWLING LEAGUE CHAMPIONS, 1934. In 1933, the Lloyd Automatic Bowling Alley Company located its factory at 1 East Main Street, along with the coincidental startup of the Beacon City Bowling League. The Mason's Square Club, one of 16 local competing teams, won the league's first title that season. Robert McElhany (standing, center) was the team's high scorer, along with Bud Morrison, Joe Mertz, Ray Clarke, and LeRoy Huff.

THE KNIGHTS OF COLUMBUS, 1968. Trinity Council Knights of Columbus was chartered on September 3, 1899, taking its name from the significance of the date as Trinity Sunday. The council moved to 395 Main Street in 1915 and there continued a long tradition of religious activity, family involvement, and community service. Generations fondly recall its second-floor bowling alleys and active Catholic Youth Organization program. Trinity Council sold the building during urban renewal and moved in 1975 to new quarters on Townsend Street.

EARLY ORGANIZED BOYS' BASEBALL, 1951. Jesse Dingee, Beacon's chief of police, gets ready to throw out the first ball on opening day of the Police Athletic League (PAL) baseball season at Hammond Field. PAL baseball was the precursor to both Babe Ruth and Little League Baseball (which began in 1952) in Beacon. That it was a simpler time is evident: team uniforms were unnecessary, and even Earl Hewes, superintendent of schools (standing next to the boys) showed up on this hot July day.

BEACON HIGH VARSITY BASKETBALL, 1963. Arguably some of the best basketball players ever to wear the Beacon High blue and gold were on the 1963 and 1964 recording-setting squads coached by Tom Winterbottom (right). In those two years, the Bulldogs went undefeated in regular season play while compiling a 37-game winning streak. Pictured with their coach, from left to right, are team stars Ed Zwinscher, Ralph Valentine, Curt Stewart, Bob King, Mike McCray, and Mickey Reed.

76

HOMETOWN HEROES, 1981. In the 50-plus years of Beacon Little League Baseball, only one all-star team has ever accomplished what these players did: a New York State championship. Along their run of 10 straight finals victories, the Beacon Little League all-stars of 1981 also captured the admiration and affection of their city. Their homecoming parade was described by county executive Lucille Pattison as "the most joyous, spontaneous, enthusiastic crowd I have ever witnessed."

A CINDERELLA SEASON, 1989. Mayor Jim Fredericks suitably declared June 25 through July 1, 1989, as Beacon High School Girls' Softball Week in honor of the 14 members of the team that claimed Beacon's first and only New York State softball championship. Led by coach Frank LoFaro, the girls amassed an incredible 26-game season record of 329 runs while holding their opponents to just 104 runs. Signs denoting their accomplishment, and Beacon's obvious pride, stood at the city limits for years following the victory.

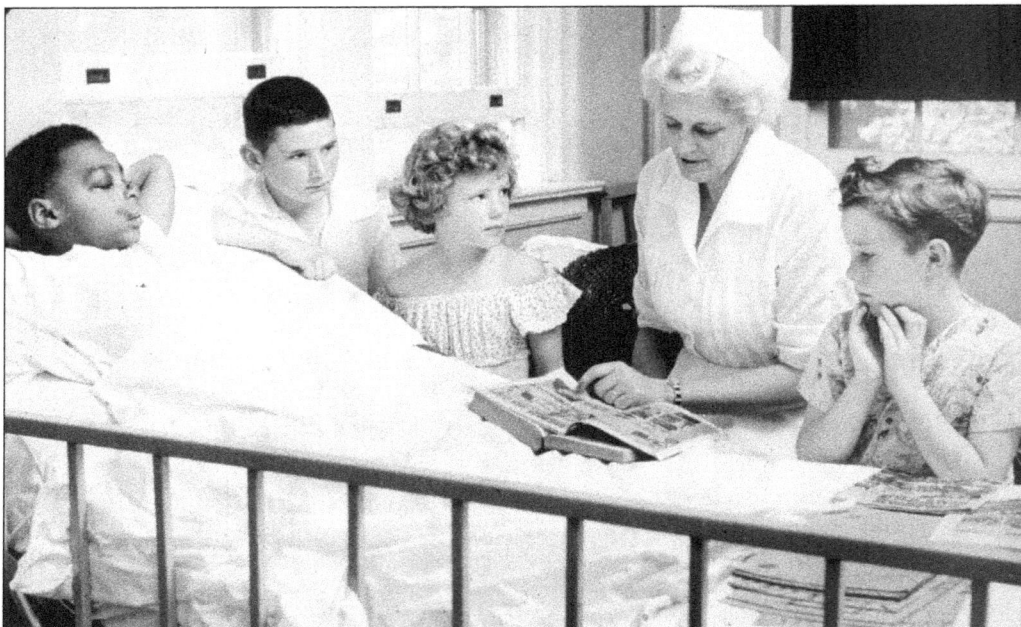

HIGHLAND HOSPITAL, VERPLANCK AVENUE, 1956. The original three-bed Highland Hospital was founded in 1871 and housed in an extant home on Russell Avenue. Helen Tompkins, wife of Lewis Tompkins, led the committee to construct a new, larger, and more modern hospital on Verplanck Avenue, which was occupied by 1902. Gertrude Balfe served as its superintendent from 1918 until 1955, during which time two additions expanded the facility. Shown are nurse Ruth Pendleton and her young patients.

HIGHLAND HOSPITAL, DELEVAN AVENUE, 1962. Highland Hospital packed up and moved patients and equipment to its third and final home on a 10-acre parcel on Delevan Avenue on March 5, 1960. The new 68-bed, $1.4-million facility was built, in part, with federal funds, although a considerable amount was raised from public subscription. The public rallied unsuccessfully to save the hospital when it fell into poor financial health in the mid-1980s, before it was sold to St. Francis Hospital of Poughkeepsie to become an alcohol-treatment center.

THE NEW MUNICIPAL BUILDING, 1964. At Beacon's old "overcrowded firetrap" city hall, one reportedly could not even get something as private as a marriage license without everyone knowing about it. By special referendum, Beacon voters agreed to an official building upgrade, and on June 13, 1964, a new $209,000 municipal building was dedicated. Mayor Stanley Odell declared that 1964, with the opening of a new disposal plant, a new incinerator, and a new city hall, would be "an outstanding year in Beacon's history."

THE NEW MUNICIPAL BUILDING, 1996. By 1987, officials in Albany considered Beacon's crowded and outdated city court facilities, housed on the second floor of the police station, to be the worst in the state, with many petitioners having to wait outside in the parking lot until their cases were called. A volunteer committee was formed to construct a new police and court facility, in which the city hall offices would ultimately also be incorporated. It still took a decade before the new municipal building (built at a cost of $5 million) was dedicated on November 15, 1996.

THE NEWSROOM OF THE BEACON NEWS, 1928. Newspapers have been an uninterrupted part of Beacon's recorded history since 1851, when the *Fishkill Standard*, a weekly, was first published. Another milestone in local newspaper history came in 1927, when Frank Gannett bought the *Fishkill Daily Herald* and the *Beacon Journal* and combined them to form the *Beacon News*. The new Beacon News building on Main Street (now the Alps Candy Shop) soon followed in 1929. Beacon lost its last daily newspaper, the *Hudson Valley News*, on August 26, 1992.

A PARADE FOR ST. JOHN'S SCHOOL, 1909. The Ancient Order of Hibernians, the Catholic societies of Fishkill Landing and Matteawan, and their counterparts from Newburgh were all escorted along Main Street to lay the cornerstone of the new parochial school of St. John's on Willow Street on April 25, 1909. St. Joachim's School had been educating pupils since 1861, and the two schools merged in 1990. The final bell of June 2001, however, ended more than the school year; Beacon's tradition of Catholic education, which had stretched back to the Civil War, concluded when the Archdiocese of New York shuttered the institution, despite a healthy enrollment.

Six

PORTRAITS

"Profiles; a likeness of a person."

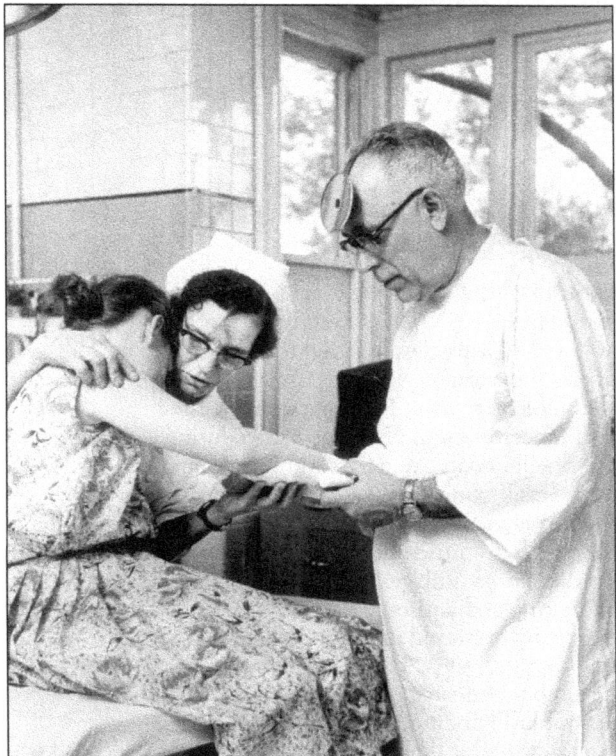

DR. DONATO ASTONE CHECKING A PATIENT. From broken bones to general surgery, Dr. Donato "Tony" Astone, it seemed, could handle any presented medical emergency or malady. After returning as one of only nine surviving members of the 42nd Rainbow Division during World War I, the life of a small-town doctor likely had great appeal for Astone. His wife, Reba Astone, was probably equally well known to the patients who streamed through the office during nearly 50 years of medical practice, as she often served as a nurse and office manager. The Astones were also regarded as stalwart community volunteers, who donated enormous amounts of time to benefit many Beacon organizations.

LT. SAMUEL LEITH, 132ND NEW YORK VOLUNTEERS, C. 1865. Samuel Leith left his butcher shop in Fishkill Landing in 1861 to fight for the Union. By the time he returned home four years later, his experience included spending 13 months in rebel prisons after being wounded and captured in the Battle of Bachelor's Creek. While in prison, Leith had his bank notes exchanged for Confederate money, with which he bought food to share with his starving comrades. His son William Leith was a local ballplayer who pitched one game in the major leagues for the Washington Senators in 1899.

GEN. HENRY E. DAVIES, C. 1865. Gen. Henry E. Davies, a veteran of more than 40 Civil War battles, was said to have had 15 horses shot from under him, though he was wounded only once. He became the trusted staff officer of Gen. Philip Sheridan during the Shenandoah campaign and was promoted to the rank of major general for gallantry at the Battle of Sayler's Creek in Virginia. After the war, he returned home to his law practice in Matteawan Village. In later years, he took up writing and authored *General Sheridan,* a biography of his old commander. His uncle was Charles Davis, a mathematics professor at Columbia University and West Point, who at his Fishkill Landing home once entertained English novelist Charles Dickens.

Sgt. John "Jack" O'Donnell, 1918.
Surrounded and trapped by the German army in the Argonne Forest of World War I, the soldiers of New York's 77th Division made their heroic five-day stand against all odds. They are now immortalized in military history as the "Lost Battalion." Amazingly, eight of that famed 1,000-member group came from the Beacon-Glenham area: Jack O'Donnell, Tony Stella, George Walker, Harold Post, Ralph and Walter Chase, Edward Ireland, and Gordon Heroy.

Peter, Joe, Romolo, Louis, and John Stella, the 1950s. The Stellas were typical of Beacon families, first- and second-generation Americans who served both their country and their community well. Romolo "Tony" Stella (center) fought in World War I as part of the legendary "Lost Battalion," and Peter and Louis Stella, who served in World War II, co-owned the L & P Restaurant in Beacon. Joe Stella was a detective-lieutenant in the Beacon Police Department, and John Stella drove for the Pizzuto Bus line.

CPL. EDWARD BURKY BACK HOME, 1945. A soldier's service and duty to his country during World War II often meant years of separation from his family. When Edward Burky was drafted in April 1943, he was only 18; his niece, Linda Murphy, was still a baby. In the late summer of 1945, after serving 19 months in North Africa and Italy in the Signal Corps of the Army Air Forces, Burky returned home to Beacon and was greeted by his three-year-old niece.

CARMINE RAMPUTI, 1944. Nineteen-year-old Carmen Ramputi, who had pleaded with his mother to sign his enlistment papers because "this country is worth fighting for," was proud to be part of the famous 4th Marine Division, first to go directly from boot camp to combat and first to capture Japanese territory. "I'm in a great outfit and the Japs know it. They will be quitting as soon as we hit the beach," he wrote to his parents before the invasion of the Marshall Islands. On February 1, 1944, a Japanese sniper targeted the boy from Beacon. He was buried in St. Joachim's cemetery with full military honors in 1947.

THE WOLCOTT AVENUE HONOR ROLL, C. THE 1940S. During World War II, some small neighborhoods in Beacon, like this one on lower Wolcott Avenue, showed their patriotism and support for the war effort by displaying the names of area boys in service on an honor roll board. From left to right, Lou Pettorossi, Henry Cucci, and Ray Thomaselli point to their names, included among dozens of others on the Wolcott Avenue Honor Roll, as Connie Yanarella looks on.

D-DAY PRAYER SERVICES AT DUTCHESS TOOL, JUNE 6, 1944. Thousands of Beacon residents went to local churches on Tuesday, June 6, 1944, Invasion Day, to pray for Allied forces invading France. Many of Beacon's factories doing vital defense work could not interrupt production lines by taking time out for special services. Instead, companies like Dutchess Tool, which was making telemotors for steering apparatus for Liberty ships, held a five-minute prayer service at 11:00 a.m. to remember those men fighting at Normandy.

THE MATTEAWAN HIGH SCHOOL BASKETBALL TEAM, 1908. James "Vince" Forrestal (seated center) was not a star on his basketball team, scoring only two field goals in five games his senior year. As a scholar, he made better use of his skills. He was editor of the school paper, the *Orange and Black*. After attending Dartmouth and Princeton, he became a reporter for the *Matteawan Journal*.

FORRESTAL CONGRATULATING ADM. WILLIAM F. HALSEY, 1945. Born in Matteawan in 1892, James V. Forrestal (second from the left) recalled of his childhood that "there were no luxuries. A 25-cent ticket to the circus once a year was difficult to come by," but he also credited his Irish immigrant father with instilling his appreciation for the fundamental value of hard work. Forrestal, who served as Pres. Franklin Delano Roosevelt's secretary of war and then became the nation's first secretary of defense, was himself credited with turning American factories into an economic war machine to achieve Allied victory in World War II.

THE COMMISSIONING OF THE USS FORRESTAL, 1955. The super aircraft carrier *Forrestal*, at that time the U.S. Navy's mightiest warship ever built, was commissioned on October 1, 1955, in Portsmouth, Virginia, with members of the late James V. Forrestal's family and Beacon Mayor Henry Kennelly (below, second from the right) on hand. It was fitting that Forrestal (right) was memorialized with a military battleship. An enthusiastic amateur boxer in his youth, who presumably never shied from a fight, Forrestal forever sported a broad, flattened nose as the result of a broken nose suffered in the ring.

BUCK SGT. LEO PIETROFORTE, 1948. Enlisting for a two-year tour in 1948, Leo Pietroforte expected to be home on South Brett Street for the Christmas of 1950. The North Korean army had other plans when it surrounded his U.S. Marine Corps unit at the Chosin Reservoir for a year of the conflict's heaviest fighting, including one of the coldest winters on record, with temperatures reaching 30 degrees below zero. The marines were eventually pushed back to the sea, and Pietroforte still recalls his relief at the sight of the USS *Black* waiting to take him to safety. Nonetheless, he was not discharged until 1952.

PVT. ANTHONY SCALZO: KILLED IN KOREA, 1952. Pvt. Anthony Scalzo was a member of Company B, 223rd Infantry Regiment of the Army's 40th Infantry Division. He died from wounds received in combat on December 30, 1952, in the "Punchbowl" area of North Korea, the only Beacon soldier to die in that war. He was the son of Salvatore and Eleanor Scalzo. "Notification of Anthony's death," the *Beacon News* reported, "was received on the same day the family received a letter from him. The letter was written Christmas Eve."

BEACON'S BRAVEST BOYS.
The youngest of the men from Beacon
killed in Vietnam was 18; the oldest
23. All of them are remembered and
honored for their sacrifice:

Sp5c. John J. Bennett, age 23, of 48 Barrett
 Place, killed March 2, 1970;
Pfc. Emilio Rivera, age 18, of 178 Main Street,
 killed October 30, 1969;
Seaman William R. Phillips, age 22, of 20
 Water Street, killed March 23, 1968;
Pfc. James S. Pittman, age 19, of 139 Main
 Street, killed October 16, 1966;
HC/2 Phillip R. Mattricion, age 23, of 45
 North Chestnut Street, killed April 5, 1967;
Sgt. Terrence E. O'Neil, age 21, of 8 North
 Cedar Street, killed May 23, 1968.

KILLED IN VIETNAM. Phillip R. Mattricion
(above), a U.S. Navy hospital corpsman,
second class, was on his second tour of
duty in Vietnam with the 3rd Marine
Division when he was killed in action
on April 5, 1967. He was 23 years old.
He had attended St. John's School and
Beacon High School. Sgt. Terrence O'Neil
(left) died on May 23, 1968, of wounds
received in combat in Vietnam. He was 21
years old. A member of the U.S. Army's
198th Infantry Brigade, he was awarded
the Bronze Star and the Purple Heart
posthumously. He was also a graduate
of St. John's School and Beacon High
School, class of 1965.

PHEBE VAN VLACK DOUGHTY AT VASSAR COLLEGE, C. 1895. After college, Phebe V.V. Doughty, M.D., Beacon's first woman physician, intended a career in education, not medicine. However, the untimely death of her older brother, Thomas, a doctor who had assisted in their father's practice, prevailed over her teaching aspirations. After further study at Cornell University and the University of Michigan, she joined her father in the family practice in 1904, becoming one of the first female doctors in the county.

A PAINTING BY ALICE JUDSON. One of the foremost female artists of the 1920s and 1930s, Alice Judson was a familiar figure to local residents who often saw her painting local scenery. Some of her best known work includes *Haystacks* at Glenham and *Lengthening Shadows* at Cold Spring. "[T]he true expression of her genius is in her marine oils, with strokes as bold and assured as those of the master marine painter, Winslow Homer," wrote one critic. Judson's Forge Studio was located on Tioronda Avenue, walking distance from her home on Leonard Street.

A JEWISH WOMEN'S GROUP, C. 1925. Just five years after they had first begun meeting in various temporary locations, 30 Jewish families dedicated their Beacon Hebrew Alliance synagogue on Fishkill Avenue in 1929. Major improvements and expansions were made to the *bimah* (altar) area and other portions of the building in 1950. Beacon has long benefited from the leadership of its prominent Jewish citizens, including Samuel Beskin, a merchant and mayor.

HELEN DOLSON, BEAUTY QUEEN. Claiming the local beauty title of Miss Mount Beacon in 1934 was only the beginning for Beacon's prettiest drum majorette. Helen Dolson, 19, also defeated more than 100 other beauties from across New York and was named Miss Empire State of 1934, earning the right to compete in the Miss Atlantic States Competition (where she was chosen as first runner-up). Each year until her death in 1991, she attended, as an invited guest, the Miss America Pageant in Atlantic City, New Jersey.

RALPH TOMPKINS, THE 1870S. Young Ralph Tompkins, perched atop a cart crafted to promote the Dutchess Hat Factory, certainly created a memorable image to promote his father's business empire in this photograph, which may have been part of a hatbox label. Lewis Tompkins is the man who made hat making synonymous with Beacon manufacturing; his three factories, Dutchess Hat, Tioronda, and Hudson Straw, employed thousands.

BENJAMIN HAMMOND (1849–1931). Apart from his successful business, Hammond's Slug Shot Works, Benjamin Hammond's civic passion was for Beacon's schools and its children. He was president of the board of education for 30 years, and it was once said that he knew, by first name, half the school children of Beacon. No community servant of his time was more widely loved and respected. At his funeral in 1931, the schools were let out early so the children could pay their respects to Beacon's "Grand Old Man."

THE MEN WHO BUILT BEACON. If a home in Beacon was built sometime in the first half of the 20th century, chances are one of three men, Henry Forrestal, James Lynch, or John Cruz, had a hand in its construction. All three were independent contractors with separate businesses in town. Lynch and his Lynch-Dutchess Lumber Company built hundreds of homes, many of them in the 1950s streets north of Verplanck Avenue. He also built some of Beacon's most recognizable buildings, such as the Matteawan National Bank (now Bank of New York) and the Hebrew Alliance synagogue. Forrestal had first worked for his father, James Forrestal, who built many of the houses south of Main Street. After he took over in later years, the Forrestal Company built many area schools, including St. Joachim's. Born in Lisbon, Portugal, Cruz (below) came to Beacon in the late 1920s and helped build Schoonmaker's Department Store (now Rite-Aid) on Main Street. Working through the Depression era and into the early 1940s, he built homes and commercial buildings throughout the city.

93

DILLON WALLACE AND HIS WIFE, LEILA, BESIDE HIS LABRADOR TENT, 1918. Beacon resident Dillon Wallace, author, explorer, and lecturer, was a leading authority of his day on Labrador, the Arctic Circle, and on wilderness travel in general. Author of 26 books (many of them adventure stories for boys), Wallace was best known locally as "the Chief." He was the founder of the Boy Scouts in Dutchess County and the first scoutmaster of Troop No. 1 in Beacon.

ROBERT MONTGOMERY, 1947. Born in Fishkill Landing in 1904, Robert Montgomery became a Hollywood film star of the 1930s. His father was once vice president of New York Rubber, but the family fell on hard times and young Robert took work as a laborer for the New Haven Railroad, wiping oil from the locomotives. He left Beacon as a penniless teenager in 1922 to begin a career on the Broadway stage, and in 1929, signed a contract with MGM to star in his first movie *So This Is College*. He was the first star to leave Hollywood to voluntarily enlist for military service in World War II, becoming an ambulance driver in France.

HYPNOTIST AND MAGICIAN JIMMY GRIPPO, C. THE 1940S. The Grippo brothers of Beacon, Jimmy and Jan, had highly successful careers in differing fields of the entertainment industry. Jimmy Grippo, a professional magician and early manager of Beacon boxer Melio Bettina, became the official host of both the city of Las Vegas and of Caesar's Palace Hotel and Casino there. Jan Grippo went to Hollywood, where he produced and directed more than 50 movies in the classic *Bowery Boys* series.

FRANK DONDERO, C. 1975. Every Main Street had, of course, the obligatory small-town ice-cream parlor, and Dondero's did not disappoint. Owner and operator Frank Dondero served up homemade desserts and confections from his parlor on Main Street's East End bend for decades. Dondero was a second-generation Beacon businessman. His father, August Dondero, was a successful antiques dealer who immigrated in 1872 and who was cited by local historian Morg Hoyt as the first Italian resident of the village of Matteawan.

THE BARBERSHOP AT 422 MAIN STREET, 1950. When Michael Acquaviva opened his business at 422 Main Street in 1925, he gave it the sophisticated-sounding (for a factory town) name of the Parisian Barber Shop. His three-man shop featured haircutting for both men and women, with shampoos for the ladies, too. In 1931, he furthered the trend toward urbanity in the community by opening, within the shop, one of Beacon's first public baths and showers. But Mike's Barber Shop (as most recall his establishment) is best remembered for its longevity: 50 years in the same location at the hotel. Acquaviva may be best remembered as the father of two of the best musicians ever to come out of Beacon, Nicholas and Anthony. Both brothers, whose love of music was nurtured by their father, studied at Juilliard. Nicholas Acquaviva was a pianist and composer of symphonic music. Anthony Acquaviva became a noted orchestra conductor and manager for his wife, singer Joni James.

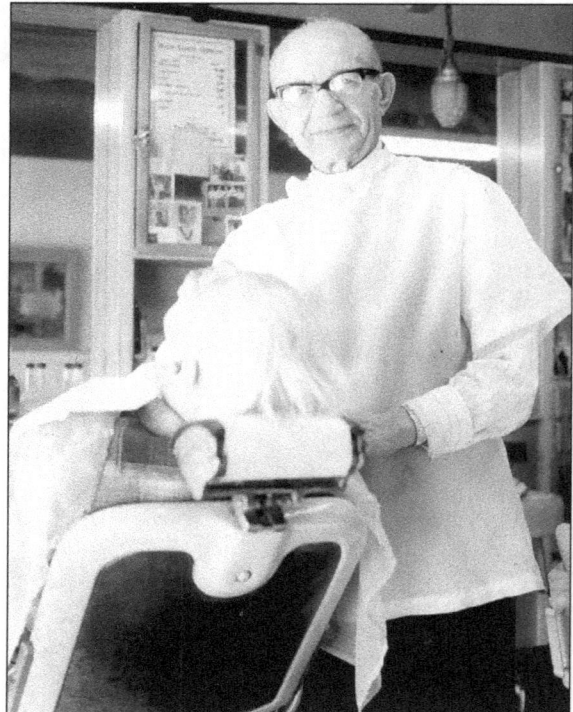

THE KIWANIS JUNIOR BAND, 1936. Among the Kiwanis Band's 42 members was a young clarinetist named Anthony Acquaviva (standing second from the right in the front), who in his adult years gained musical fame as an orchestra conductor, recording artist, and manger and producer for his wife, singer Joni James. In 1936, Acquaviva was just another musician in a talented junior band whose members marched in parades wearing white bucks and white ducks.

USIFER'S CITY BAND, C. THE 1950s. In the early 1920s, at the young age of 13, Beacon's Joe Usifer was playing in his older brother Mike's band and thrilling local concert audiences with his clarinet playing. Joe Usifer later left the band, graduated from Juilliard, joined the NBC Orchestra, and, as conductor and band director with the stage name Paul Lavalle, had his own radio program, *Band of America*. Meanwhile, Mike Usifer carried on as leader of Usifer's Band and entertained Hudson Valley residents for decades.

JIM FREDERICKS, C. 1975. Perhaps it came as little surprise to some that Jim Fredericks, a former boxing coach, would throw his hat into the political ring someday. Mayor from 1984 until 1988, Fredericks was a hometown favorite who, among other accomplishments, welcomed Ron and Ronnie Beth Sauers to Main Street's East End, thereby beginning the grass-roots movement to restore and revitalize downtown.

MAYOR CLARA LOU GOULD, 2003. Clara Lou Gould was not only the first female and longest-tenured mayor of Beacon, but also the visionary leader who helped spark the city's renaissance. Gould, a Cold Spring native who worked in the publishing industry before first running for political office in 1988, helped Beacon write a new chapter in its history as a center for the arts. During her tenure, the new city office complex was built and dedicated, infrastructure was improved, and myriad public projects were completed to revitalize the city. Pictured with her is Gov. George Pataki.

Seven

STILL LIFE

"A snapshot in time."

MATTEAWAN NATIONAL BANK EMPLOYEES, THE 1920S. Beacon's first savings institution was the First National Bank of Fishkill Landing, later Fishkill National Bank, which was incorporated in 1863. The Matteawan National Bank received its charter in 1893 and had assets amounting to $10 million when it merged with the Farmers and Manufacturers National Bank of Poughkeepsie in 1963. The full staff of the 448 Main Street branch is pictured here. From left to right are Mary Mahurter, Grace Whitney, Floyd Callahan (assistant cashier), Loretta O'Rourke, Warren Taylor, George Callahan (cashier), Muriel B. Schofield, and Emory J. Hager.

Mase Hook and Ladder's Seagraves Fire Truck, c. 1930. For years, the "Hooks" had no rig, no house, and no official recognition as a fire company by public officials. The Mase firemen in those early days were viewed by some as something akin to a comical spectacle, rushing to fires on foot with ladders on their backs. By 1911, with a handsome new firehouse on Main Street and a new motorized truck soon to follow, Mase Hook and Ladder was no longer low man on the fire pole.

Elmer Steele and the Tompkins Hose Baseball Team, 1902. Fishkill Landing's Elmer Steele (far left), who in the course of a few years pitched his way from a local firehouse team to the major leagues, began playing professional baseball with the Pittsburgh Pirates in 1910. After finishing his brief career in Boston, Steele moved to Poughkeepsie, where he umpired in local leagues and continued to play ball into his fifties.

100

JACOB WEINSTEIN (1857–1915). When Jacob Weinstein opened his barber shop in Matteawan in 1875, few had any idea the young Poughkeepsie native would spend the next 40 years serving his adopted community. Credited as the founder of Beacon Engine Company, Weinstein was its first foreman. He also chaired the village's board of health. During his funeral, the city's barbers shuttered their doors in a show of respect to a man described by his obituary as being "universally liked and respected."

BEACON'S FIRST FIRE TRUCK, 1912. The first automotive fire apparatus in town was Beacon Engine Company's Webb pumper, purchased in 1912 at a cost of $5,900. The new truck could pump 500 gallons of water a minute, reach speeds up to 45 miles per hour, and carry 1,000 feet of hose and eight men. A locomotive bell was mounted on the dashboard to be rung as a warning for horses and people to clear the way.

THE LAKE FAMILY, 1920. In Beacon's early decades, working-class families made up the majority of residents in a manufacturing community then dominated by the hat-making industry. Richard Lake (above, far right) was typical of those who were drawn here to find work. He is shown with his coworkers making straw hats at the Dutchess Hat Works on lower Main Street. Born in 1865 in Bristol, England, Lake came to America in 1883 and settled in Beacon to work as a hatter. His wife, the former Dora Leavitt, who came here from Massachusetts, could trace her ancestry back to the Pilgrims of the *Mayflower*. The Lakes (below) lived here for more than 50 years, raising 13 children in their South Cedar Street home. In 1932, at age 66 and retired, Lake applied for, and was granted, his American citizenship.

THE NATIONAL RECOVERY ACT PARADE, 1933. It was the greatest parade in the city's history, as 3,500 marchers and 10,000 spectators assembled to endorse the New Deal program that was to spur the nation's economy out of its doldrums. Pres. Franklin Delano Roosevelt had issued a call for public support of his "codes of fair competition," and Beacon responded with a blockbuster parade organized beneath the banner of the National Recovery Act (NRA) symbol of a Blue Eagle.

THE MATTEAWAN STATE HOSPITAL FLOAT, NRA PARADE, 1933. The NRA parade was a morale booster, a chance for Beaconites to dress up, have fun, and send the message "Who's afraid of the big bad wolf of the Depression?" Surely, no one in Beacon. Pete Didio, in the wolf costume, ominously circled the house of a live pig in one of dozens of floats that filled the parade, but the ballyhoo could not keep the wolf from the door; the NRA was struck down by the Supreme Court in 1935, and the Depression went on.

CHANLER'S FIFE, DRUM, AND BUGLE CORPS, 1910. October 2003 marked the 100th anniversary of the Chanler Drum and Bugle Corps, which according to *Drum Corps World* magazine is the oldest continuously active drum corps in America. The heart and soul of Chanler's today is Augustine Arquilla, who, first as a member and then as the band's leader, has had 70 years of involvement with the organization. Chanler's longevity may be best explained by Arquilla himself: "We are like a family."

THE VFW GIRLS DRUM CORPS, C. 1940. Formed in 1938, the John J. Bump Auxiliary Drum Corps was named, like its sponsoring Veterans of Foreign Wars post, in honor of a Beacon soldier killed in World War I. Assembled in front of the high school for this photograph, the 40-member, all-girl corps was led by Majorette Helen Dolson (a future Miss Empire State). A sampling of other corps members' names includes Mary Romanelli, Ann Trochan, and Madeleine Giordano.

WALKING NEAR FOUNTAIN SQUARE. In the 1870s, walking was more than a way of life; it became a pastime, with walking races to win cash purses. In Fishkill Landing, the Great 48-Hour Walking Match was held one week in January 1879, and a double-team, 24-hour walking match was held the next. Matteawan's Michael Costello once covered 13 miles in one hour, 49 minutes; he was so confident, he put up $20 to challenge any taker to keep stride with him.

A HIGH-WHEELER IN MATTEAWAN, THE 1890s. The high-wheeler became the latest craze of the Gay Nineties. Despite its cost (up to three months' wages of the average worker), the bicycle had become "an abiding national habit" by 1893 and somewhat of a local nuisance, according to a 1891 newspaper report. Cyclists "flit up and down our main streets in the dark, their tiny headlights being all that can be seen until they are close upon you. Some riders stay out to 12 o'clock at night and ride in bands."

READY FOR THE BLACKOUT, MARCH 10, 1942. Mayor Thomas Cunningham (right) and Police Chief Jesse Dingee inspect black fabric, with a slit sufficient to provide light to drive but not enough to be seen by enemy aircraft, installed on a police car by Sgt. Ralph Parker. Beacon's wartime civil defense plan marshaled the volunteer forces of 124 air-raid wardens, 107 auxiliary police, 175 firemen, 64 Red Cross drivers, scores of Boy Scouts and Girl Scouts to serve as messengers, and an entire city ready to turn off its lights to minimize enemy targets.

FOOTBALL REINSTATED AT BEACON HIGH SCHOOL, 1947. The death in 1902 of 11-year-old Hugh Schofield while playing football at recess was the reason, it was claimed, that football was banned for more than 30 years at Beacon High School. However, through the efforts of local supporters such as Henry Forrestal, football was reinstated on October 25, 1947. On that day, thousands of spectators watched coach Jim Gauriloff's team lose their home opener to Cardinal Farley High School 21-0, the first of four losses during that brief, but historic, first season.

THE PLAYGROUND AT MEMORIAL PARK, 1969. For five decades children have enjoyed summertime activities sponsored by the Beacon Recreation Commission in Beacon's parks. Memorial Park was originally called Tompkins Park, named after the property's owner, Ralph Tompkins, a member of one of Beacon's most well-known families. The park was purchased by the city in 1943 for $10,000. The money was raised by public subscription after an idea was proposed by the Beacon Elks to dedicate the Wilkes Street field as a memorial to all of the men and women then serving their country in the war.

BOB CAHILL AND HIS KNIGHTS OF COLUMBUS TEAM, 1962. In 1969, after almost two decades of involvement with youth basketball and baseball in Beacon, coach Bob Cahill (standing, far left) was about to leave sports for politics. Starting in 1951 as a coach in St. John's Catholic Youth Organization basketball and in 1954 as manager of the Babe Ruth Knights of Columbus, Cahill's teams were perennial winners and, over the years, dominated their respective leagues. As a politician, Cahill continued his winning ways by twice being elected mayor of Beacon.

THE BEACON VOLUNTEER AMBULANCE CORPS, C. 1963. A dedicated group of volunteers, led by police officer Walter Detwiller, formed the Beacon Volunteer Ambulance Corps in 1958, taking as their first home the former Sunoco Service Station on the corner of Liberty and East Main Streets. The corps expanded to a second headquarters on land donated by Highland Hospital in 1980 and named its entrance Arquilla Drive to honor faithful responder and charter member Vincent Arquilla.

THE BELL PRESENTATION CEREMONY AT FORRESTAL SCHOOL, 1953. When the old Spring Street School was about to be supplanted by the new James V. Forrestal School, a call was raised to salvage the old school's bell as a legacy from the old to the new. A Save Our Bell campaign was organized, wherein hundreds of alumni each donated $1 toward the bell's rescue and removal to Forrestal. It has now become a Forrestal tradition for each graduate on the last day of school to ring the old bell in fond farewell.

POLICE CHIEF ROBERT W. EPPS. Robert Epps joined the Beacon Police Department in 1953 as the city's first black officer, and as a man destined to be its future leader. When Mayor George Tomlinson announced that, as of May 12, 1979, Lt. Robert Epps would take command of the police department, it was greeted with citywide approval. "His reputation as a gentleman and a compassionate officer," the *Evening News* commented, "is long standing in the community." Epps, who retired in 1982, appears on the left in the third row in the 1956 photograph above and fifth from the right in the front row in the 1970 photograph below.

THE CITY FATHERS, 1956. At its formation in 1913, Beacon adopted the commissioner form of government, a system administered by five individual department heads, rather than a traditional city council. The mayor was joined by the commissioners of accounts, public works, public safety, and finance in guiding day-to-day city affairs. James A. Frost was the first mayor, and his successors included Henry Kennelly (left), pictured here with the commissioners of 1956.

THE FIRST WARD FORM OF GOVERNMENT, 1992. The Beacon City Council sworn into office on January 1, 1992, was like no other. For now, city residents were represented by one of four ward representatives, two at-large councilors, and a strong mayor, in this case, Clara Lou Gould, who made the transition between the two forms of government. Voters had supported the government change in a public referendum based upon the findings of a citizens' committee that determined the commissioner format no longer met the needs of a modern city.

110

BOB OUTER ON LOCATION, C. 1967. WBNR, so named for Beacon-Newburgh Radio, took to the airwaves at 5:30 a.m. on December 19, 1959, and has been delivering local news and programming, with a good helping of community service, ever since. Part salesman, part broadcaster, and all showman, Beacon resident Bob Outer has been a fixture at the AM 1260 station for more than 40 years.

THE USS BEACON DOCKING, 1971. A week of festivities that featured a dinner dance, a softball game (between crew members and local firemen), and hundreds of eager tourists greeted the USS *Beacon* when it docked in its namesake city in August 1971. The navy patrol gunboat (PG-99) saw active and reserve duty from 1969 to 1989, when it was transferred to the Greek navy and rechristened *Ormi*. The boat laid claim to being one of two first ships to officially fly the 1775 Union Jack in celebration of the nation's bicentennial, raised with a 21-gun salute at the navy's 200th birthday celebration in 1975.

WILLIAM H. PEARSE SPEAKING TO THE GRADUATING CLASS OF 1955. Under the stewardship of school principal William H. Pearse (standing at the piano), two generations of students passed through the halls of Beacon High School and therein received a proper education. Pearse was principal of Beacon High for an astonishing 40 years—from 1920 until his retirement in 1960. By dint of his venerable presence, Pearse's words were to be heeded, as he was not to be forgotten by the thousands he graduated.

THE NEW BEACON HIGH SCHOOL, 2003. Beacon voters overwhelmingly approved construction of a new high school in a referendum called to replace the cramped 1915 high school with a more modern facility. They certainly got just that when classes began in September 2002 in the new $32 million complex, featuring a 1,000-seat theater, 8 science laboratories, a library-media center, a television studio, an indoor pool and fitness center, and some of the most electronically sophisticated classrooms in the nation.

Eight

LOCAL COLOR

"Interest or flavor of a locality; slices of life."

BEACON HIGH SCHOOL CHEERLEADERS, 1923. Elmore "Tubby" Tallmadge (left), Harriet Ormsbee, and Roland "Cy" Whittaker comprised the 1923 high school cheerleading squad. "The first part of the year Cy Whittaker made up several peppy cheers and taught them to us at Assembly. Just watching him tear across the floor flinging his arms in the air inspired us, so that we almost raised the roof with our war hoop yells and heart-rending shrieks," proclaimed the class yearbook.

THE SARGENT SCHOOL BEEHIVE HOUSE, C. 1895. The busy activity of the young women within earned this Russell Avenue school the nickname "the Beehive House." The Sargent Industrial School for girls began operations here in 1891 to provide classes in cooking, sewing, and laundering, under the stewardship of Aimee Sargent, wife of Winthrop Sargent. By 1897, an enrollment of 200 girls prompted a move to the larger quarters of the Rothery Homestead on Schenck Avenue, where the school remained until its dissolution in 1918.

A MATTEAWAN HIGH SCHOOL CLASS, 1911. One of the lessons being taught this March day to a mixed group of 41 pupils at Matteawan High School is practical mathematics. Written on the blackboard is the following problem: "If beef loses 20 percent of its weight by roasting, find the weight of 14 pounds of roast beef before cooking." Incidentally, one of the girls in this class photograph is Helen Tallmadge Bierce, who later became a bookkeeper in the city offices and lived to be 100 years old. (The answer, by the way, is 17.5 pounds.)

THE CIRCUS COMES TO TOWN, 1910. The early decades of the 20th century were the golden age of the circus, when even small towns like Beacon might get two circuses in a year, complete with acrobats, horses, lions, and strongmen, and all for just 25¢ a ticket. Soon after these elephants paraded in front of the Dondero block in the West End, the tents would be raised in the ball field behind the post office for the grand show.

SUFFRAGETTES ON THE MARCH, 1913. "A suffrage stronghold"—that is how the *Fishkill Standard* characterized Beacon in 1913. It was little wonder, then, that a group of female activists from New York City chose Beacon for the opening scene of a three-county "whirlwind horseback tour" for women's suffrage. The crowd gathered in Bank Square, where the speakers assured all that once women had the vote, "there will no longer be crime or vice. In fact, wickedness will be unknown." Women won the right to vote in New York State four years later.

SWIMMING AT THE TREES, THE 1930S. The most popular spot to cool down in the 1920s and 1930s was a sandy stretch of beach known as the Trees, located along Fishkill Creek on the east side of Liberty Street, where the Villas condominiums now stand. This swimming spot had actually been the favorite one for generations of Beaconites. In 1932, the Kiwanis Club erected two bathhouses on the site and the city's merchants chipped in to buy a float and diving board for the ol' swimmin' hole.

HAPPY BIRTHDAY! C. 1930. The Victorians are credited with staging the first children's birthday parties and dressing up young mistresses and masters in their very best birthday attire for elaborate celebrations. The formality continued well into the first decades of the 20th century, when young neighbors like these on Russell Avenue—all dressed in their Sunday best—gathered to wish Gordon Ticehurst a happy birthday. After World War II, birthday parties—like the rest of modern life—became more casual.

A VOX-POP BROADCAST AT THE BEACON THEATRE, 1948. VOX-POP, the popular 1940s radio program featuring "the voice of the people from coast to coast," made a live broadcast from the Beacon Theatre in March 1948. Beacon resident Kim Barrett entertained listeners and the sold-out crowd with his "old mountaineer" stories, earning an easy chair, two pipes, and a portable radio for his prize. Three local youngsters, Danny Keenan (seated, right), Marty Bradley, and Tom Healey, were each presented with a bicycle for their participation.

THE BEACON BEARS, 1931. The Wilkes Street athletic fields were once home to the semiprofessional Beacon Bears football team, which had played sporadically before World War II but formed again in 1945 to post winning seasons in 1947, 1948, and 1949. In 1948, the squad rewarded 4,000 fans with a thrilling 19-13 victory over Haldane. The advent of television in the 1950s meant locals could catch the New York Giants games at home each Sunday, and the Beacon Bears slowly disbanded. An estimated 100 players had donned the black-and-gold uniforms of the Bears during their nearly 20 years of play.

BEACON POLICE AS KEYSTONE KOPS, 1950. The annual Halloween parade became a ritual from the very first Masquerade March of 1935, when a $5 first prize was awarded to the best costume. In the years to follow, the parade stepped off from Bank Square at 7:00 p.m. sharp and proceeded up Main Street to the municipal building. The fun culminated at the Beacon High School gym, where the Lions Club handed out doughnuts and ice cream. The Halloween tradition reached its zenith in the early 1950s, when more than 1,500 marchers turned out. By the 1960s, it had disappeared.

DAVE MOHURTER AND HIS TIN MAN CREATION, 1950. In every Halloween and firemen's parade of the 1940s through the 1960s, the Tin Can Symphony could be heard clanking and clanging as the tin-can men were pulled along by truck, but seemingly marched in unison. These tin figures, made out of empty motor oil cans, were the whimsical creations of Dave Mohurter, a local auto mechanic whose home hobby brought delight to thousands of Beacon parade goers.

THE MEMORIAL DAY PARADE, 1950. The American Legion honor guard steps off in one of Beacon's longest-running civic traditions: Memorial Day observances. Annual commemorations have long included a parade and wreath-laying ceremonies at the Memorial Building, which was built to thank the soldiers of World War I. Each year, a wreath is tossed into the waters of the Fishkill Creek from the East Main Street Bridge in memory of Beaconites who lost their lives at sea.

A PARADE PASSING THE 260S BLOCK ON MAIN STREET, 1951. In a preview of what was to happen to Beacon during urban renewal in the late 1960s and 1970s, this entire Main Street block of small shops and second-story apartments was razed to make room for a new supermarket plaza in 1956. The dramatic makeover of this section of Main Street was completed that year with the opening of the Empire Market. Over the years, the supermarket changed owners and names to the Grand Union and now to Key Food.

A MINSTREL SHOW AT THE ROOSEVELT THEATRE, 1950. Representing the best in local talent, singer Harriet Sandford DiRocco performs the musical number "I'm in the Mood for Love," at the Presbyterian Men's Club Blackface Minstrels of 1950 at the Roosevelt Theatre. Minstrel shows, popular throughout the Hudson Valley in the first half of the 20th century, were considered wholesome entertainment by contemporary audiences. By the early 1960s, with the advent of the Civil Rights movement, black face revues disappeared as an acceptable form of theater.

CHRISTMAS CAROLERS, 1956. The December 24, 1956, edition of the *Beacon News* reported that the members of the paper's night staff had been "pleasingly surprised" to hear young voices singing "Silent Night" in good harmony outside their Main Street offices just a few days before Christmas. The strains emanated from these six youngsters, from left to right, Linda DiRocco, Thomas DiRocco, Diane Alonzo, Remo D'Alatri, Pat Ratigan, and Joe Stofan.

YOUNG BANKERS, 1956. A whopping 83 percent of Ruby Lyons' third-grade class at South Avenue School participated in a youth savings program sponsored by the Beacon Savings Bank in 1956. Their efforts were captured for posterity in this photograph, which was part of a time capsule placed in the bank's lobby floor and meant to be opened in 25 years in 2001. Building renovations kept the capsule inaccessible for an extra year, but when finally opened, it revealed the compounded human interest due to these young savers.

DRIVE-THRU BANKING, 1956. Beacon Savings Bank offered residents the most modern of conveniences when it unveiled Beacon's first drive-thru banking window on the city's birthday: May 15, 1956. Open beyond traditional lobby hours, the window was part of an increasing trend of a society on the go. Though the identity of the first mobile patron was unfortunately not recorded with this photograph, the names of treasurer Emory J. Hager, teller Ann Brown, and president Sherwood Robinson were duly noted for posterity.

THE JUBILEE CELEBRATION, 1963. It was a grand celebration of civic pride, one that commemorated 50 years as a young and promising city. Storefronts, streets, and homes were decorated; dignitaries were invited; an official souvenir program was produced. The Beacon Golden Jubilee events of 1963 were administered through an incorporated entity that sold shares of "Jubilee stock" to finance a week's worth of fun and pageantry, including Homecoming Day and Industry Day.

THE JUBILEE BURIAL AT THE ELKS CLUB, 1963. A Jubilee souvenir plate, Jubilee booklets, a Jubilee banner, hats, bonnets, bow ties, and even Jubilee wooden nickels were made. Never before or since has so much gala memorabilia for the city been collected nor so much community pride (and fun) been raised than as was on display in Beacon's Golden Jubilee celebration. In the spirit of good fun, even Mr. Ray-Zor was laid to rest by the Brothers of the Brush.

JUBILEE QUEEN JANET VAN SLYKE, 1963. Beacon Mayor Stanley Odell places the crown on Janet Van Slyke, queen of Beacon's Golden Jubilee, at opening day ceremonies on June 1, 1963. The queen and her court of nine princesses held reign over the city's week-long celebrations, which included the dramatic *Pride and Progress*. The queen also received a royal prize: a week's vacation for two in Bermuda.

THE NABISCO FLOAT IN THE JUBILEE PARADE, 1963. The Saturday-to-Saturday celebration of Beacon's golden jubilee taking place in the first week of June 1963 culminated in a grand firemen's parade on June 8. City officials estimated that between 10,000 and 20,000 people lined the streets that day. The National Biscuit Company's float, featuring a golden birthday cake in honor of the city, was a particular crowd favorite, especially when Nabisco employees handed out samples of company treats.

THE START OF THE SOAPBOX DERBY, THE 1960S. Roll down Verplanck Avenue in a homemade hot rod in a winning time of 30 seconds or less and the prize of a new bicycle was yours to be had at the finish line of the Kiwanis Club's Soapbox Derby. During late August in the 1950s and 1960s, hundreds of spectators lined the course, which started just west of the Cross Street intersection, to cheer on the young racers at this annual event.

THE CAR WASH OPENING, 1969. Leaving his new wife behind in Italy and unable to speak any English, Luigi DeDominicis (second from the right) proved that Beacon still offers every resident willing to work and sacrifice an opportunity to achieve the American Dream. Arriving in 1954 to take welding work at today's Fishkill Correctional Facility, DeDominicis set out in his own blacksmith business within a decade. By 1968, he built his Main Street car wash, just one of many properties he eventually developed.

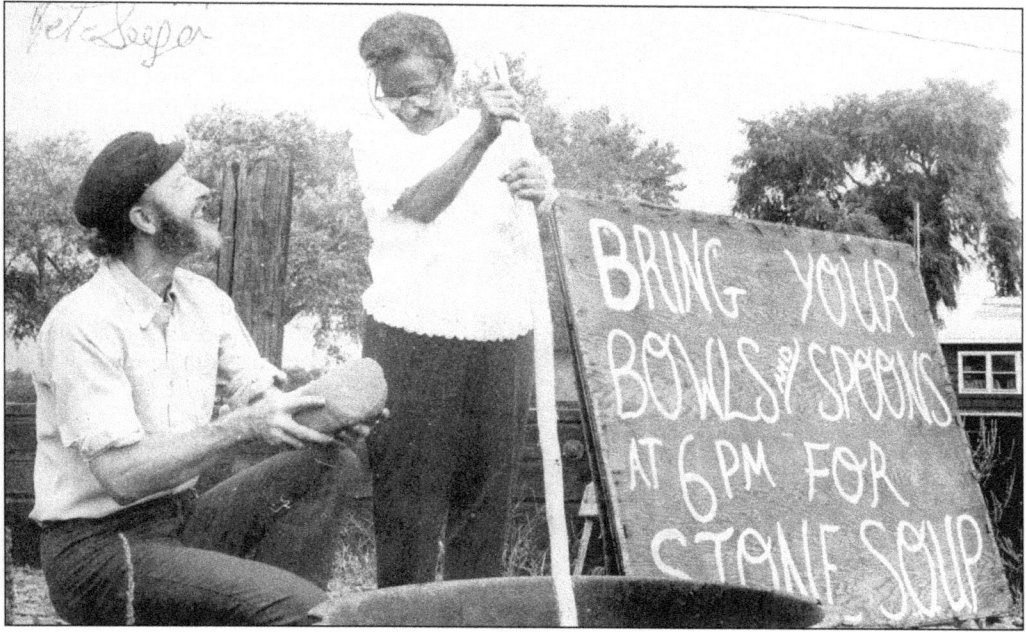

Pete Seeger and Catherine Quill Preparing Stone Soup, 1971. Who would have thought that the mix of food and song were the key ingredients to the making of a cleaner Hudson River? The Sloop Club festivals of the 1970s, featuring Beacon resident and folk singer Pete Seeger, ignited a local environmental movement to save the Hudson by attracting people to the river with a blend of music and seasonal farm crops of strawberries, corn, pumpkins, and, of course, stone soup.

The Sloop Club Pumpkin Festival, 1975. This one group of dedicated individuals single-handedly has changed the image of Beacon's waterfront for the better. Working out of an old ferry diner as their clubhouse since 1969, the Beacon Sloop Club's mission has been to attract people to the river by annual, seasonal events, whether they are harvest festivals or free sailing on the sloop *Woodie Guthrie*. Beacon's Riverfront Park, the fairy tale-comes-true story of a city dump transformed into a city park, is only one contribution of many the club has made to our city.

THE NEW YORK STATE SEAL. According to Joseph Gavit's *New York History*, Volume XXXI, the seal of the great state of New York features the sun rising behind Mount Beacon. "The shield symbolizes in the full sun the name and idea of Old York and the old world; the mountains, river and meadow, with the ships, convey the name and idea of New York in the new world," Gavit wrote. The seal was first designed as a coat of arms for the state in the 1850s and was adopted as the permanent state seal in 1885.

THE HISPANIC FLOAT IN THE SPIRIT OF BEACON DAY PARADE, 1976. Back in 1977, after a stormy period of racial unrest and violence broke out among Beacon's youth, community leaders and concerned citizens sought a way to promote harmony within the city. The consensus was to create a community day, on which Beacon's ethnic and cultural diversity would be celebrated with a parade, food booths, exhibits, and entertainment. Now, Spirit of Beacon Day is celebrated as an annual tradition on the last Sunday in September.

DIGGER PHELPS AND HIS FAMILY ON PARADE, 1974. One of Beacon's most famous sons, Fordham University and University of Notre Dame basketball coach Digger Phelps, who is one of the winningest coaches in college basketball history, regularly returns to his hometown, which eagerly changed the name of the street of his boyhood home from Cottage Place to Digger Phelps Court in his honor. Although christened Richard, he is known universally as Digger due to his family's longtime business as local undertakers.

THE FILMING OF NOBODY'S FOOL, 1992. Lights, camera, action! Well, actually, inaction on the part of Beacon residents, who stopped whatever they were doing to watch the filming of the Academy Award–nominated film *Nobody's Fool*, starring Paul Newman, Melanie Griffith, and Bruce Willis. Filmed largely along the streets of the East End and in a private home on High Street, the movie featured several cameo roles by city residents and plenty of footage of Beacon's building stock.

ACKNOWLEDGMENTS

We would like to acknowledge the many people who have donated photographs and information regarding the community's history to the Beacon Historical Society through the years. In particular, we express gratitude to those who helped in the creation of *Beacon Revisited*, including, but not limited to the following:

Fred Antalek, Filly Baisley, Moe Baxter, the city of Beacon, Beacon Engine Company, Beacon Police Department, Julius Boccia, Royal Bogardus, Betty Carey, Carmine Ramputi Marine Corps League, Central Hudson Gas & Electric, John Darcy, Maureen Darcy, Dia:Beacon, Matt Dondero, Francis Doughty, Derry Dubetsky, John Fasulo, Nancy and Larry Gallagher, Duane Galletta, Clara Lou Gould, Charlotte Haug, James Kelliher, Phillip Mattricion, Pat and Tom Moore, Gloria Mulia, Diane Murphy, Robert W. Murphy, the Newburgh Historical Society, Margaret Provost, Nancy O'Neill, Bob Outer, Scott Plumer, the *Poughkeepsie Journal*, Ron Samuelson, Ronnie Beth and Ron Sauers, Ramona Scalzo, Scenic Hudson, Kathy Schetter, Dick Shea Archives, Wanda Sramek, Eileen Steffanci, Judy Stella, Douglas Story, Janice Sullivan, Paul Tesoro, Tallix Art Foundry, Gordon Ticehurst, Joan Van Voorhis, Vernie Way, Janet Williams, and Bruce Wolfe.

RALPH MORSE (1911–2000). The Beacon Historical Society and, in fact, all of Beacon owes a debt to Ralph Morse, who chronicled the city's past and progress through the lens of his camera, often on behalf of his beloved Beacon Engine Company. Morse left a priceless gift in the form of his photographs, and his spirit will live on as long as future generations appreciate their value.

www.ingramcontent.com/pod-product-compliance
Lightning Source LLC
Chambersburg PA
CBHW080558110426
42813CB00006B/1335